# IN FOCUS

# NICARAGUA

A Guide to the People, Politics and Culture

*Hazel Plunkett*

**LATIN AMERICA BUREAU**

INTERLINK BOOKS
NEW YORK

© 1999   Hazel Plunkett      All rights reserved.
First published in 1999

**In the U.S.:**

Interlink Books
An imprint of Interlink Publishing Group, Inc.
99 Seventh Avenue, Brooklyn, New York 11215 and
46 Crosby Street, Massachusettts, 01060

**Library of Congress Cataloging-in-Publication Data**

Plunkett, Hazel
   Nicaragua in focus: a guide to the people, politics and
   culture / by Hazel Plunkett.
         p. cm.   (In focus guides)
   Includes bibliographical references.
   ISBN: 1-56656-286-4  (pbk)
   1. Nicaragua - Guidebooks.  2. Nicaragua - Description and
   travel  I. Title
   F1523.5.P68   1999
   917.28504'54 - dc21                           99-19668
                                                     CIP


**In the U.K.:**

Latin America Bureau (Research and Action) Ltd,
1 Amwell Street, London EC1R 1UL

The Latin America Bureau is an independent research and publishing
organization. It works to broaden public understanding of issues of
human rights and social and economic justice in Latin America and the
Caribbean.

A CIP catalogue record for this book is available from the British Library

ISBN: 1 899365 36 2

*Editing*: Marcela López-Levy
*Cover photograph*: Jenny Matthews/Format
*Cover design*: Andy Dark
*Design*: Liz Morrell
*Cartography and diagrams*: Kees Prins and Marius Rieff

**Already published in the *In Focus* series:**
Argentina, Belize, Bolivia, Brazil, Chile, Colombia, Costa Rica, Cuba,
Dominican Republic, Eastern Caribbean, Ecuador, Guatemala, Jamaica,
Mexico, Nicaragua, Peru, Venezuela

Printed and bound in Korea

# CONTENTS

# INTRODUCTION: THE EYE OF THE STORM

On October 30, 1998, Hurricane Mitch tore into Nicaragua, causing the worst natural disaster of the twentieth century. Days of torrential rains and winds of up to 200 miles an hour laid waste to vast expanses of the country. Thousands of people died, entombed in mudslides or drowned as rivers broke their banks and flooded towns and villages. Roads, bridges, houses, crops and animals were swept away. In a desperate attempt to escape the violence of the water, people climbed trees and clung to the roofs of their homes.

More than a week later, hungry, cold and often sick, the majority of survivors were still waiting for help to arrive. Although relief workers on loan from foreign governments soon joined the emergency operation, they came too late for some people, who, exhausted by their ordeal, died before assistance reached them. A team of Cuban doctors, experienced in disaster relief work, was refused entry by President Alemán, who said that Nicaragua had more than enough medical expertise to cope with the situation.

Disease spread rapidly as decomposing bodies and rotting animal flesh contaminated the water supplies. In the final count, as many as 3,000 people died as a result of Hurricane Mitch. More than a fifth of the population were stranded in refugee camps, their homes and livelihoods destroyed. Damage was estimated at over $1 billion and it was anticipated that rebuilding the country would take decades.

Nicaragua has had more than its fair share of disasters, and Mitch is just the latest in a long line of tragedies which have befallen its citizens. In 1972 the capital Managua was all but destroyed by an earthquake. Lonely stretches of wasteland and the ruins of hotels, shops and offices, which characterize modern-day Managua, are a reminder of the city's former vitality. The old cathedral is collapsing into the main square which, but for the annual July celebrations of the country's 1979 revolution, stands empty. Beyond the square, the plastic roofing and makeshift homes of the capital's poorest citizens are growing ever closer.

In Nicaragua, the old is slowly giving way to the new. But the scars of the country's turbulent history are never far away. Nicaragua is marked by the struggle to retain its independence, first from the colonizing Spanish, then from the United States. U.S. influence began conspicuously when the American adventurer William Walker invaded the country and declared

Managua's cathedral, ruined in the 1972 earthquake.          *Robert Francis/South American Pictures*

himself president in 1856. The U.S. has since supported numerous armed interventions to safeguard its political and economic interests.

In the 1920s an anti-imperialist movement was founded by Augusto Sandino to break U.S. dominance. Although its success in winning back Nicaraguan independence was short-lived, the victories of his guerrilla army are legendary. Even today a wooden cut-out of Sandino towers over the Inter-Continental Hotel in Managua. Following his treacherous assassination in 1934, Nicaragua was plunged into forty years of repression and violence as the dictatorship of Anastasio Somoza took hold, with U.S. support.

Throughout the capital and the country's towns and villages, monuments commemorate the tens of thousands of men and women who died fighting the tyranny of Somoza's regime. His overthrow in 1979 by the National Sandinista Liberation Front (FSLN) brought Nicaragua to prominence worldwide. Daniel Ortega, the revolution's fatigue-clad leader, the poets and priests in his cabinet, the female military commanders all attracted international coverage as did the literacy, health care and land reform programs. But it was the outbreak of a proxy-war with the United States that really propelled Nicaragua into the political limelight.

Caught up in the enmities of East-West *realpolitik*, Nicaragua's attempts to redistribute land and wealth unleashed a hostile response from the U.S., which financed and armed the Contras, a counter-revolutionary force. The war still stirs powerful emotions and continues to divide Nicaraguans. Although a peace agreement was eventually reached in the late 1980s, it came too late for the revolutionary Sandinista government, which was voted out in 1990 by a nation desperate to end the war.

Today Nicaragua quietly embraces the politics, economics and culture of the United States. Billboards which carried the revolutionary health messages of the 1980s have been replaced by advertisements for mobile phones; Sandinista murals have been painted over; and workers' co-operatives have been superseded by free trade zones. Since the Sandinista Party was defeated in the 1990 elections, two successive right-wing governments have pushed through economic reform programs that have opened the country to the vicissitudes of the world market.

Nicaragua's president in the late 1990s was Arnoldo Alemán, who beat Daniel Ortega in the 1996 elections, and took up the challenge of modernizing Nicaragua. As an enthusiastic supporter of market economics, he hoped to revive the country's flagging economy through foreign investment and gave special attention to tourism and the long-cherished dream of a railway linking the Atlantic and Pacific oceans. Yet the modest economic growth figures recorded before the onslaught of Hurricane Mitch were achieved at the price of growing inequalities between the rich and poor. Wealth was further concentrated in the hands of a small elite as Nicaraguans returned from the U.S. to set up businesses and reclaim property confiscated by the Sandinistas, while the majority lived in poverty and without work.

Hurricane Mitch destroyed the foundations of Nicaragua's recovering economy in a matter of days and rendered the government's plans for regeneration largely meaningless. Indeed, the scale of the disaster moved world leaders, (though not hardened bankers), to accept a moratorium on its debt repayments and consider writing off some of the money the country owed. The task of reconstruction will demand fresh energies, enormous patience and a spirit of cooperation, if Nicaragua is to set its sights on the long-term goal of renewal.

This guide will examine the history, politics and economy of Nicaragua, including its crucial and difficult relationship with the United States. As the country leaves its revolutionary past behind, and enters a testing period of recovery, Nicaragua In Focus reflects on where Nicaragua stands today.

# 1   HISTORY: TYRANNY AND REVOLUTION

## Pre-Columbian Days

As the ancestors of modern Nicaraguans fled the lava flows of a massive volcanic eruption, which took place more than 10,000 years ago, their footprints were perfectly preserved under the falling ash. Today they take pride of place in a small museum in the neighborhood of Acahualinca, a densely populated and desperately poor area of Managua, Nicaragua's capital. After this first record of life, historians have traced the earliest established civilization back to 2000 BC. Living on the Pacific coast and in the central highlands, this people's culture and language were probably influenced by the Aztec and the Maya kingdoms to the north. Nahuatl was widely spoken, remnants of which are found in the Spanish of present-day Nicaragua. Although archeologists have not yet uncovered physical evidence which would provide significant insights into the culture and politics of the early settlements, it is known that cocoa was used as the monetary unit and that, in common with today's inhabitants, the staple foods of its people were maize and beans.

When the Spanish colonial empire expanded into Nicaragua in the early sixteenth century, the conquistadors encountered three indigenous groups: the Nicaindios, the Chorotegano and the Chontal. Chiefs known as *caciques* presided over established and thriving agrarian states. Often at war with one another, they did not unite to resist the Spanish incursions. Indeed, some opted for friendly relations with their invaders. An expedition led by Gil González Dávila in 1522 established a settlement in the area controlled by the Nicaindios between Lake Nicaragua and the Pacific. Chief Nicarao, their despotic ruler, apparently welcomed the conquistadors and was peacefully converted to Christianity. Thereafter the colonization of the interior began. A counter-attack led by a rival Indian leader, Chief Diriángen attempted to return the territory into indigenous hands, but the bows and arrows of his men were no match for the firearms of the Spanish. Although his soldiers failed to hold back the colonizing forces, their resistance is now a celebrated part of Nicaraguan history.

## Colonial Rule

The Spanish conquistadors consolidated their hold over the territory, which they called Nicaragua after Chief Nicarao and *agua*, the Spanish word for water. They incorporated it into their Central American empire known as the Kingdom of Guatemala, which also included the provinces of Costa

Rica, El Salvador, Guatemala and Honduras. Largely neglected by the Spanish Crown, Nicaragua was ruthlessly governed as a semi-autonomous unit. Its representatives invariably engaged in violent power struggles as they set about accumulating as much wealth as possible. Disappointed by the province's small reserves of gold and silver, the Spanish authorities concentrated on shipping slave labor to the rich mines of Panama and Peru. The trade had a devastating effect. In just forty years of Spanish occupation the indigenous population fell from one million to 30,000 people. They died in the service of the conquerors, mistreated and malnourished or from diseases brought from Europe. Others chose to end the misery of their lives by committing suicide.

The Spanish became concerned about the province's rapidly dwindling work force on economic grounds and attempted to curb the worst examples of exploitation. Nevertheless, a system of tributes and forced labor, known as the *encomienda*, was maintained throughout the colonial period. In return for obligatory religious instruction, Indians were required to undertake work without pay and make gifts of maize and beans to individuals as well as government officials. Although the indigenous population was not totally destroyed, the ethnic composition of Nicaragua was permanently changed. The *mestizos*, the mixed-race offspring of the colonizers and Indian women, grew rapidly in numbers. Only a small number of communities succeeded in retaining their Indian identity as the activities of missionaries and enforced Christian teaching sought to ensure their conversion. By 1821, when Spanish rule ended, the Catholic Church was well established throughout the towns and villages on the Pacific coast of Nicaragua, an influence which still prevails today.

### The Mosquitia Kingdom and British Influence

The Spanish did not attempt to extend their occupation of Nicaragua beyond the Pacific, as they believed the Atlantic Coast was poor in mineral resources. They were also wary of the small number of Indian groups living in the sparsely populated expanse of rainforest, which cut off the Atlantic Coast from the rest of the province. Even so, their ships did have to navigate the Rio San Juan, an important waterway connecting the Atlantic Coast and Lake Nicaragua. It was here that they were often attacked by English buccaneers, who used the creeks and lagoons of the eastern coast as safe havens from their piracy on the open seas. The frequency of the raids increased in the seventeenth century when the British empire expanded into the Caribbean and established trading posts on the Atlantic Coast of Nicaragua.

Looking at petroglyphs, Maderas volcano *Robert Francis/South American Pictures*

With the support of the Miskito, a group of Indians who had intermarried with escaped African slaves, the British were able to operate on the Atlantic Coast with relative ease. In return for their loyalty, the Miskito were given guns and ammunition, which they used to assert their dominance over the Sumo and Rama Indians of the region. Traders forged a special relationship with a Miskito chief, who was eventually crowned 'King Jeremy I' in 1687 by the governor of Jamaica. Although Nicaragua was effectively divided into two, it was not until 1740 that the 'Kingdom of Mosquitia' was officially placed under the protection of the English Crown. The region did not generate huge wealth for the early British settlers, but in addition to a modest trade in timber, sugar and Indian slaves, there were lucrative spoils from the looting of Spanish ships. However the attacks petered out following an agreement between England, Spain and France at the end of the seventeenth century, which put a stop to the illegal activities of buccaneers.

British aspirations to conquer the Spanish province intensified in the late eighteenth century when the construction of an economically important trans-Nicaraguan canal, linking the Pacific and Atlantic coasts, was seriously contemplated. In 1780 British forces set out to capture the towns of Granada and León, the two centers of Spanish colonial power. Although they ransacked some of the Spanish fortifications, they were eventually forced to retreat, defeated by heavy rains and lack of supplies. With a youthful Horatio Nelson, who would later become Lord Admiral of the British navy, they retired to Bluefields, their stronghold on the Atlantic coast. Not long after, under the terms of the 1783 Treaty of Paris, the British were forced to withdraw from the Atlantic Coast and allow the Spanish to take control of the area.

In the absence of their British allies, Miskito power on the Atlantic Coast diminished. Although they refused to submit to Spanish rule and deposed the appointed regional commander of Mosquitia, a new threat was emerging. The creoles, the descendants of white settlers and their African slaves, began to challenge Miskito economic and political domination of the Atlantic Coast. Swelled by the influx of Afro-Caribbeans arriving from Jamaica, the English-speaking group was favored by the British, who resumed formal control over the Miskito protectorate in 1840, shortly after the departure of the Spanish from Central America. Their return, however, proved short-lived. Under pressure from the United States, which began to play a more active role in the region, the British signed the Treaty of Managua in 1860 and abandoned their claims to the Atlantic Coast. British settlers were evacuated and a protected reserve for the Miskito was established. At the same time, the Rio San Juan and the Caribbean ports of San Juan del Norte and Puerto Cabezas were removed from Miskito control, which marked the beginning of a decline in their influence.

### Independence and American Intervention

At the turn of the nineteenth century, a rise in nationalist sentiments throughout the New World threatened Spanish colonial rule. The mestizo and creole elite gradually undermined Spain's administration of the provinces of Central America, and after a short war in 1821 they claimed their independence. Although the provinces initially joined the Mexican Empire, they broke away and formed a federal state in 1823. Split by rivalries between different economic interests, separate republics eventually emerged. Nicaragua declared itself independent in 1838.

The political life of the new country was dominated by a violent conflict between the Conservatives and the Liberals. The former represented the interests of the traditional landed classes and were opposed to the liberalization of trade. The Liberals, in contrast, supported the opening up of markets and attracted a following among farmers and merchants. Their power bases were established in Granada and León respectively. Similar factions existed elsewhere in Central America, and their troops regularly arrived to fight alongside their political allies in Nicaragua.

William Walker

*Courtesy of South American Pictures*

These internal conflicts were extremely damaging to the prospects of Nicaraguan independence, as they left the new nation open to the interference and intervention of foreign powers. As a country providing a potentially strategic trade link between the Pacific and Atlantic seaboards, Nicaragua was particularly vulnerable to exploitation. The United States was swift to take advantage, and so began its long and controversial involvement in the history of modern Nicaragua. In 1849 it signed a treaty with Nicaragua, agreeing to provide protection against aggressors in return for the exclusive rights to build a canal, and Commodore Cornelius Vanderbilt, an American businessman, was given the contract for its construction. When the British condemned these plans and moved to threaten the project militarily, the U.S. decided to enter into a joint venture with Britain, which it did without consulting the Nicaraguan government.

Although the U.S. and Britain had made a deal which aimed to satisfy both their commercial interests, the dispute over the inter-oceanic canal rumbled on. In 1823 the Monroe Doctrine had outlined American intentions to assert regional authority and end European involvement in Central America, which it considered its "sphere of influence". The arrival in 1854 of U.S. gunboats in San Juan del Norte at the mouth of the Rio San Juan and the bombardment of the British-controlled town was a very clear demonstration that the U.S. was willing to use force to achieve its policy aims. Meanwhile, the Conservatives and Liberals were still locked in a battle for domestic control and appeared unconcerned about the U.S. contempt for Nicaraguan sovereignty.

In an attempt to gain the upper hand, the Liberals invited William Walker, an American adventurer, and his mercenaries to help oust the Conservative government in Granada. Walker sailed into Nicaragua and forced the Conservatives to surrender before installing a puppet president, whom the U.S. immediately recognized. Soon after, Walker arranged his own appointment as the country's ruler, holding fraudulent elections in 1856. He proposed the annexation of Nicaragua to the U.S. and the reintroduction of slavery, which had been abolished in 1834. Nicaraguans across the political divide were outraged by his actions, and united to take on his troops. The task of expelling Walker, known as the "National War", was protracted and finally ended in the southern town of Rivas. Under attack from soldiers drawn from the Central American republics, he was rescued in 1857 by the U.S. marines. It was the British navy which eventually captured Walker and handed him over to Honduran authorities, who put him in front of a firing squad.

The experience of the "National War" brought the armed conflict between the Conservatives and Liberals to an end, and a period of relative calm and co-operation followed. The inter-oceanic canal was never built and the route was eventually closed in 1868, although plans for construction survive to this day. Renewed political upheaval in 1893 put General José Santos Zelaya, the son of a wealthy coffee producer, in power. His dictatorship survived for sixteen years, during which time he opened the country to foreign investment and developed its infrastructure. The Atlantic Coast was also reincorporated into Nicaragua and renamed Zelaya, despite the reluctance of its inhabitants. The strident nationalism and foreign policy of the Zelaya government also upset U.S. business and political interests. In 1909, when the U.S. marines were sent in to support Conservative forces rebelling against Zelaya, the production of coffee, bananas, gold and timber was almost exclusively owned by American companies. In 1912 the Americans returned again to restore order following a Nicaraguan uprising and they remained, with the exception of nine months, until 1933.

### Sandino and Nicaraguan Nationalism

The persistent meddling of the U.S. in the internal affairs of Nicaragua gave rise to widespread popular discontent. The U.S. government supported rapidly expanding American business interests and so-called "dollar diplomacy" began in earnest. In a series of treaties, starting with the Dawson Accords in 1911, a compliant Nicaraguan administration relinquished total financial control to the U.S. In return for a modest loan, a group of three U.S. government nominees and one Nicaraguan were appointed to manage the economy. American companies were consequently exempted from taxation and received other benefits, which helped boost their already healthy profits.

The rising political influence of the U.S. reached its apogee when it secured the right to select the country's presidential candidates. In the 1916 elections, U.S. marines guarded the polls, ensuring that the small group of enfranchised Nicaraguans voted in line with American interests. Such disregard for the country's sovereignty and independence enraged a growing number of people, who despaired at the failure of their political leadership to resist U.S. interference. In the absence of any serious politi-

U.S. soldiers display the flag of rebel leader, Sandino, 1932                    *CORBIS*

cal opposition, a nationalist force took shape with the aim of expelling the American military presence from Nicaraguan territory.

The force was led by General Benjamin Zeledón, a former member of the Zelaya government, who organized a peasant uprising in 1912. It was crushed by the marines, but his death at the hands of the Americans inspired others to turn to arms. Augusto Sandino, a mechanic from the small town of Niquinhomo, near Managua, set about building a guerrilla force from the mountains of Las Segovias in northern Nicaragua. Rural workers, who had been displaced when American companies, including United Fruit, took over vast expanses of land to cultivate coffee, bananas and other produce for export, were enthusiastic recruits. Forced to work more marginal and less productive land, they were attracted by Sandino's commitment to social and economic justice. Their military campaign, which started in 1927, targeted U.S.-owned businesses and proved highly successful. Marines stationed in Nicaragua were unable to prevent Sandino's troops, who became known as Sandinistas, from occupying most of central, northern and eastern Nicaragua by 1931. The Americans used planes in bombing raids for the first time in the Western Hemisphere, attacking the northern border town of Ocotal, but the Sandinistas remained defiant.

In the face of Sandino's increasingly powerful patriotic army, the U.S. government took the decision to withdraw the marines as a means of calming the situation and reducing anti-American feeling. Instead it would exert its influence through the indigenous defence force, the National Guard, which was less likely to antagonise patriotic Nicaraguans, but would remain subservient to their interests. The U.S.-negotiated peace in May 1927 between the warring Conservative and Liberal forces had specifically agreed to the U.S. taking command of and training the National Guard, the country's constabulary. Anastasio Somoza, an ambitious young Liberal and a favourite with the U.S., rose quickly through the ranks and became the first Nicaraguan Chief of the National Guard.

The U.S. marines left Nicaragua in 1932, despite a request from Anastasio Somoza that they stay to help defeat Sandino's army. Meanwhile Juan B. Sacasa, elected president in the same year, declared his willingness to negotiate with Sandino. In talks in early 1933, a peace agreement was signed and Sandino's troops laid down their arms after six years of fighting and the loss of more than 20,000 lives. Yet the National Guard had become a law unto itself and continued to harass the Sandinistas. Rumours of a coup also abounded, and whilst President Sacasa refused the protection offered by Sandino, he agreed to reform the National Guard. On February 21 1934 under orders from Anastasio Somoza, Sandino was abducted and assassinated after a presidential dinner in Managua.

### The Somoza Dictatorship

Sandino's assassination was a telling indication of the ruthless ambition of the man who became Nicaragua's most hated dictator. Somoza amassed ever more power, outmaneuvering his opponents and wielding complete control over the Nicaraguan armed forces. A campaign of terror against Sandino's followers, who kept up the fight after his murder, removed any possibility of their regrouping to threaten Somoza's ascendancy. After a series of puppet presidents, Somoza eventually installed himself as Nicaragua's new leader on January 1, 1937. He ruled with extreme violence, deploying the National Guard to intimidate and murder opponents. He also skilfully retained his supporters' loyalty through a system of corruption and bribery, which never allowed any rival to build a power base. Those who dared resist the edicts of his regime risked imprisonment, torture or death. Prisons, such as El Fortín in León, which is still standing today, serve to remind all Nicaraguans of the cold brutality of the dictatorship.

Although Somoza did not tolerate any opposition, he was careful to maintain the pretense of a democratic system. Elections were held on a regular basis, but were rigged. Two political parties, both created by Somoza, participated in a parliament: the ruling National Liberal Party

Anastasio Somoza (son)    *Hulton Getty*

and the National Conservative Party, which became known as the "loyal opposition". Efforts were also made to portray the activities of parliament as meaningful, although the deputies were essentially powerless and acted on the orders of the dictator. Somoza did not ride roughshod over the Nicaraguan constitution, but found loopholes or engineered legislative changes. To get around the prohibition on a second consecutive presidential term, he temporarily installed a stooge before returning to office.

This charade of a Western liberal democracy was acted out largely for the benefit of the U.S., an ally of crucial importance to Somoza. Their relationship was founded on a mutual interest in power. Nicaragua backed U.S. foreign policy in the international arena and provided political and logistical support for numerous American interventions elsewhere in the region. Somoza even went as far as to volunteer members of his National Guard for combat in Korea, an offer declined by the Truman administration. In return for his allegiance, the dictator received sophisticated weaponry, which he used to maintain domestic control. Members of the National Guard and his two sons, who were being prepared for power, also attended military academies in the U.S.

The Somoza family rapidly accumulated personal wealth on such a vast scale that some commentators dubbed Nicaragua "Somoza Inc". Its members owned most of the country's gold and silver mines, sawmills, factories, cattle ranches and cotton estates, whose profits were dramatically increased by the strategic use of state funds to build roads and ports necessary for their export. Somoza's fortunes were also boosted by the confiscation of properties belonging to Germans and Italians during the Second World War, when he took a pragmatic decision to set aside his fascist beliefs and lend support to the Allies.

Despite repression by the Somoza regime, opposition forces dared to organize. Although protests, largely attended by students and workers, were put down ruthlessly, support for a clandestine movement against the dictatorship grew. There were armed attacks staged by former Sandino followers and even attempts on Somoza's life from within the discontented ranks of the National Guard. The poverty and hardship inflicted by the regime on the majority of Nicaraguans were accentuated by the international economic crisis of the 1930s and 1940s. In 1944 people took to the streets and participated in massive demonstrations. Initially Somoza listened to their demands, wary of U.S. reaction to a full-blooded assault on the crowds. As the hostilities of the Cold War escalated, anti-communism provided the mantle under which he unleashed the repression needed to retain control of the country.

The myth of Somoza's invincibility was finally broken when a poet named Rigoberto López Pérez walked into election festivities in León and shot him at point blank range. He was immediately flown to Panama but, despite the efforts of U.S. surgeons, died on September 28, 1956. His two sons Luis and Anastasio continued to run the country, clamping down on dissident elements more brutally than ever. Hatred of the Somozas and their despotic rule increasingly united Nicaraguans.

It took a natural disaster to expose the greed and callousness of the Somoza family to the international community. In 1972 a huge earthquake devastated Managua, killing an estimated 30,000 people and making tens of thousands homeless. When Luis and Anastasio pocketed the emergency aid from abroad, they succeeded in alienating even upper-class families. Support for the Somoza dynasty was collapsing. The introduction of martial law in 1974 only hastened its downfall, and perhaps more importantly, provided the window of opportunity for the formation of an altogether more effective opposition movement.

### Insurrection and the FSLN

The *Frente Sandinista de Liberación Nacional*, (FSLN), the National Sandinista Liberation Front, was formed in 1961 by Carlos Fonseca, Tomás Borge and Silvio Mayorga in Tegucigalpa, the capital of Honduras. It began as a relatively small political and military organization, inspired by the Cuban revolution. Armed attacks launched by the FSLN on the National Guard in the 1960s were sporadic and rarely successful. Ironically, the defeat of a Sandinista unit at Pancasán in northern Nicaragua in 1967 marked a positive change in the guerrillas' fortunes, despite the loss of leading Sandinista combatants, including Silvio Mayorga. News of a daring assault on the National Guard circulated widely and the bravery of the resistance fighters captured people's imaginations and encouraged more people to join the struggle.

While the number of recruits to mountain training camps increased, the process of consolidating the FSLN's presence in the towns and the

Portraits of Sandino and Carlos Fonseca, founders of the FSLN    *Tony Morrison/South American Pictures*

countryside was slow. Political education was painstakingly and clandestinely carried out amongst the peasantry and urban workers with the aim of building a mass movement. Gradually people were encouraged to organize trade unions and local neighborhood committees. In 1969 the FSLN published its "Historic Program", which stated its commitment to removing the Somoza family from power by force. It set out a framework for a future revolutionary government, guarantees on individual political, civic, economic and social rights and promises of land reform, education and health care.

By the early 1970s, the FSLN guerrillas were more effectively organized and their operations against the National Guard became increasingly successful. Specially trained units carried out a series of daring operations. In one raid on a party held by the Minister of Agriculture in 1974, a group of prominent politicians and a number of relatives of the Somoza family were held hostage. The FSLN extracted a high price for their release, forcing Anastasio Somoza, who was now ruling the country, to pay a ransom of $5 million and to free fourteen political prisoners, including the future president of Nicaragua, Comandante Daniel Ortega. In response to the growing strength of the guerrillas, counter-insurgency measures were tightened up still further. The National Guard terrorized, killed and tortured Sandinista sympathizers and the FSLN was weakened by the loss of some important leaders.

Internally the FSLN struggled to contain ideological divisions and during the course of 1975 three distinct and independent factions emerged. The "Prolonged People's War" advocated building the resistance movement from guerrilla bases in the countryside, while the "Proletarian Tendency" concentrated on creating a vanguard for revolution among urban workers. The "Third Way" or "Insurrectionists" proposed a dual strategy of supporting the liberation struggle and integrating the progressive middle class into a broad alliance of opposition forces led by the FSLN. The Ortega brothers, Daniel and Humberto, were proponents of the "Third Way", which gained influence as members of the traditional middle-class as well as intellectuals gradually came out in support of the FSLN.

### Revolutionary Women

During the insurrection, women played a vital role in undercover activities, and a number emerged as important guerrilla leaders. Like their male colleagues, they carried AK-47 rifles and dressed in combat fatigues. Luisa Amanda Espinosa, Claudia Chamorro and Arlen Siu were among the thousands who risked and lost their lives for the FSLN. Others went on to serve under the Sandinista government as community activists, politicians and government officials.

One of the most prominent women guerrilla leaders was Doris Tijerino, who joined the FSLN in the early 1960s and worked with Carlos Fonseca, one of its founding members. She is best remembered for her part in the often-recounted defense in 1969 against an attack on the safe house of Julio Buitrago, a member of the FSLN directorate. The operation was televised by Somoza as a demonstration of his regime's power, but badly backfired when the FSLN guerrillas were caught on camera bravely singing the Sandinista hymn as a force of 400 troops advanced with the support of aircraft and a Sherman tank. Buitrago and four other revolutionaries were killed. Doris Tijerino and one other were captured and subsequently tortured by the National Guard.

In 1978 Dora María Tellez, known as Comandante 2, helped take 49 deputies hostage in a spectacular raid on the National Palace. Somoza was forced to agree to the demands of the FSLN, and 58 Sandinista prisoners were released, among them Doris Tijerino and Tomás Borge, another founder of the FSLN.

After the triumph of the 1979 revolution, Tijerino became the Head of Police and was at that time the only woman in the world to be in charge of a national police force. Dora María Tellez became the Minister of Health.

The pressure on Somoza did not just come from the left-wing guerrilla movement. In January 1978, Pedro Joaquín Chamorro, the right-wing editor of *La Prensa*, one of the country's largest newspapers, was assassinated by Somoza's henchmen for his part in bringing together conservatives and liberals opposed to the regime. More than 50,000 people immediately took to the streets of Managua calling for an end to the dictatorship. The U.S. attempted to persuade Somoza to step down and pushed for the creation of a new government that would exclude the FSLN, but by this time the revolution was unstoppable. A wave of popular unrest was sparked throughout the country, a situation the Sandinistas used to their advantage. The FSLN made a final big push and towns throughout the country fell one by one. On July 19, 1979, television footage was broadcast around the world depicting the victorious Sandinista troops marching triumphantly into Managua. The National Guard maintained its bombing campaign until the bitter end, causing extensive damage to the infrastructure of the country and claiming a huge number of lives. The shell of a retreating plane, shot down by the FSLN, can still be found on a hillside on the outskirts of Condega in the north of the country, a bitter reminder of the terror of the Somoza era.

### The Revolution at War

The enormous task of building a new democratic state awaited the Government of National Reconstruction, which although led by the FSLN, was comprised of representatives from a wide political spectrum, who had participated in the overthrow of the dictatorship. Some 50,000 people had sacrificed their lives in the revolutionary struggle and tens of thousands more were injured in the fighting. From the ruins of war and near bankruptcy, the work of reconstruction began immediately. People set about clearing the rubble of destroyed buildings, restoring water supplies and preparing land for agricultural production. Enthusiasm and expectations of improvements in their lives ran high.

The revolutionary government gave priority to the basic economic and social needs of Nicaraguans. A National Literacy Crusade launched in 1980 took 100,000 volunteers into the countryside, giving people the opportunity to learn to read and write for the first time in their lives. Within a year the illiteracy rate fell from 50 to 13 percent. Free education became available as primary and secondary schools were built. Medical students and hospital staff were recruited to vaccination and health campaigns. They taught people about the causes of disease and promoted preventive activities such as cleaning wells, building latrines and clearing mosquito breeding sites. Health indicators improved dramatically: infant mortality was halved, polio was eradicated and other infectious diseases were reduced. In 1983 the World Health Organization declared Nicaragua's emphasis on prevention and education a model for developing countries.

As a predominantly rural country, revitalizing Nicaragua's farming sector was essential to the health of its people and economy. Rural development was an urgent priority for the FSLN, as the war against Somoza's National Guard had brought agricultural production to a halt. In particu-

Adult literacy class, 1981

*Mike Goldwater/Network*

lar, Nicaragua needed to become more self-sufficient in food. Initially the government was forced to rely on imports, until the longer-term plans for expanded production were implemented. Under the dictatorship, access to land was denied to the majority of people, who were employed as wage laborers and therefore unable to grow their own produce. The Sandinista agrarian program, which redistributed land and provided credit and technical assistance, dramatically increased the production of maize, rice and beans, the staple foods in Nicaragua. The FSLN also remained committed to a mixed economy which enabled large and medium-sized private producers to stay in business, earning the country valuable foreign exchange. The policy of supporting wealthier farmers caused dissatisfaction among the peasantry.

A series of land reforms, which remain a highly controversial political issue today, were the centerpiece of the Sandinista revolution. They reversed the gross inequalities in ownership affecting half of the country's arable land and benefited almost two-thirds of rural families. In the first phase, the assets of the Somoza family, which made up a fifth of the country's cultivated land and a quarter of its industrial sector, were confiscated and transferred to state farms and cooperatives. Collective working was not necessarily popular with many peasants, who aspired to owning their own land and working for themselves. Under pressure to meet their demands, a second phase of reforms expropriated some large and unused farms. But the distribution to individual farmers was slow and came too late to prevent some peasant farmers joining a counter-revolutionary movement, which was being organized by former members of Somoza's National Guard.

## Counter Revolution

The FSLN considered the National Guard members who fled to Honduras to be the last vestiges of *Somocista* resistance. They were few in number and posed no serious threat to Nicaraguan security. The fortunes of these exiles were to change dramatically, however, with the election of Ronald Reagan as U.S. president in 1980. An ardent and obsessive anti-communist, he made it his personal crusade to ensure that the Contras, as the counter-revolutionaries became known, were supported. Using the pretext of alleged FSLN gun-running to the Farabundo Martí National Liberation Front, a guerrilla army in El Salvador, the CIA was authorized to equip and train the Contras. Between 1981 and 1986, $100 million was officially transferred to fund their insurgency activities. Real expenditure was considerably higher, boosted by funds secured through secret weapon sales to Iran, a scandal which later became known internationally as the "Iran-Contra affair".

The huge amount of money and the training provided by the U.S. transformed the Contras into a force capable of waging war on the revolution. At its height, it was a loosely co-ordinated body with 15,000 men from politically diverse backgrounds. The largest group within it, the Nicaraguan Democratic Front, was run by former National Guard members and was joined by a growing number of peasants, some of whom were forcibly recruited. The brutality with which they tortured and killed their prisoners is well documented by Amnesty International and Americas Watch. On the Atlantic Coast some smaller armed Miskito Indian groups formed, in response to the serious political mistakes the Sandinista government made in their region, to fight for independence. Another important counter-revolutionary force was led by Edén Pastora, a once celebrated guerrilla leader, who defected from the Sandinista government and moved to Costa Rica.

Despite the Contras' sophisticated weaponry and U.S. advisors, they failed to establish a base within Nicaragua or take the fighting beyond the mountains and into the towns. But the threat of an American invasion hung over the Sandinista government throughout its administration. U.S. troops in neighboring Honduras were regularly exercised along the Nicaraguan border and provided the Contras with logistical support and intelligence on the movements of the Sandinista army. The CIA also assisted in a series of sabotage operations, including the mining of the Pacific port of Corinto in 1984, an action for which the U.S. was subsequently found guilty by the International Court of Justice at the Hague.

On a war footing, the FSLN government was forced to divert precious resources away from the social sector and into the defense of the country. Between 1984 and 1988 more than half of the national budget was spent on maintaining the armed forces. In addition, a fifth of the economically active population was enrolled into the Sandinista army, following the introduction of compulsory conscription in 1983. The Contra War lasted for almost nine years, during which Nicaragua suffered enormous human losses and extensive damage to its economy. The need for a peaceful resolution to the conflict became increasingly desperate as the death toll rose. Of an estimated 60,000 casualties, a third were civilians working as farmers, teachers or medics in the war zones.

The day-to-day existence of the majority of Nicaraguans became ever more precarious. The massive loss of life and the tough conditions in which civilians lived undermined support for the revolution. The country grew visibly poorer and food was rationed. Revenues from the country's most valuable exports underwent a dramatic slump as a result of decreased production due to the war and falling international commodity prices. The U.S. trade embargo, which was put in place in 1985, also contributed to the country's economic problems, depriving Nicaragua of its traditional export and import market. Although alternative trading partners were found, the shift took up the valuable time and energy of the Sandinista government. In the meantime, farms and businesses using U.S. machinery were suddenly unable to obtain spare parts, and consequently struggled to work to capacity.

### The Peace Process

The toughest challenge faced by the Sandinista government throughout the 1980s was to strike a balance between carrying out its revolutionary program and defending the country. The war increasingly took priority, stalling plans for social improvements. Peace required that the U.S. abandon its aim of destroying the revolution, a policy goal which seemed beyond the realms of Sandinista power. President Ortega sought to promote international support for a peace process from the outset of hostilities, but it was not until the mid-1980s that the energy devoted to resolving the conflict diplomatically began to pay off. In 1984 the presidents of Colombia, Mexico, Panama and Venezuela met to discuss a disarmament plan for Nicaragua. In a series of regular meetings, the "Contadora Group" as it

Voting queue, Boaco                                    *Paul Smith/PANOS Pictures*

became known, developed several proposals. The U.S. proved the stumbling block on each occasion as it either refused to participate or took part only to undermine the initiatives.

Nevertheless, support for a negotiated peace grew as the illegality of the U.S. involvement in Nicaragua was exposed. In 1986 the Iran-Contra scandal broke, exposing the role of the White House in the secret sales of arms to Iran and the resulting funding of the Contras. The Reagan administration was guilty of both circumventing its own Congress and violating international law, a transgression later confirmed by a ruling of the International Court of Justice against the U.S. Political changes in Central America also helped create an atmosphere for dialogue. In Guatemala and Costa Rica, recently elected presidents were especially anxious to restore stability to Central America and tackle the region's economic crisis. Under the leadership of Oscar Arias, the President of Costa Rica, a regional peace initiative was signed by all five Central American countries on August 7, 1987 in Esquipulas, Guatemala.

The plan, which called for the withdrawal of foreign advisors, a ceasefire and democratic elections, was welcomed internationally, except by the U.S. The Bush administration renewed funding for the Contras and fighting in Nicaragua continued. Despite U.S. intransigence, President Arias was awarded the Nobel Peace Prize in 1987 for his efforts in promoting an end to conflict in Central America, and the American policy of intervention in Nicaragua looked increasingly shaky. The Sandinista government seized the opportunity offered by widespread criticism of the U.S. to demonstrate its commitment to peace, and announced its willingness to make further concessions.

In a statement in October 1987 the Sandinista government declared that it was willing to begin peace talks with the Contras through the mediation of Cardinal Obando y Bravo, the head of the Catholic Church in Nicaragua. Over 1,000 former National Guard members imprisoned since 1979 were pardoned and released, and a series of amnesties were announced. Thousands of counter-revolutionaries, demoralized by the war, immediately chose to disarm and return home. An agreement between the Sandinista government and the majority of the Contras followed in March 1988, in which they would hand over their weapons in exchange for a resettlement deal and elections. A meeting of the Central American presidents in February 1989 gave the Contras 90 days to disarm, but few guns were given up before the country went to the polls in February 1990.

### From Bullets to Ballots
The campaign leading up to the elections was a nervous and tense affair. Despite signing peace accords, the Contras held on to their arms and increased their attacks. Their cause was helped by $50 million of so-called humanitarian aid from the U.S. Allegations that the Sandinistas would rig the result abounded. The opposition parties, including the United National Opposition (UNO), a coalition of 14 parties, and political commentators world-wide were ready for a decisive FSLN victory. An enormous surprise awaited them. On February 26,1990, following a count watched by more than 1,000 international observers and the world's media, UNO was declared victorious with 54.7 percent of the vote. The FSLN trailed with just over 40 percent.

A visibly shattered Daniel Ortega conceded defeat. In a moving speech, he reminded people that the Sandinista Party had built the institutions for democracy in Nicaragua and stated that its elected members would take up their seats on the opposition benches in the National Assembly. The country went into profound and lasting shock. For days the streets of Managua remained almost empty as UNO supporters stayed at home, either lacking the enthusiasm for public celebration or fearful of Sandinista reprisals. The unthinkable had happened and Violeta, the widow of Pedro Joaquín Chamorro, assassinated by Somoza, took over as Nicaragua's first woman president. Her election marked the first peaceful transfer of power from government to opposition in Nicaragua's history.

# 2    POLITICS - REVOLUTION IN REVERSE

Political graffiti daubed on buildings, bridges and roadsides is ever-present in Nicaragua. Even the earliest hand-made stencils of "El Comandante" Daniel Ortega dating back to the early 1980s survive on the walls of houses, whose occupants are rarely able to afford a paint job. But the images of youthful guerrilla leaders brandishing AK-47s and the red and black of the FSLN are gradually disappearing under the logos of more recent arrivals to the political landscape. The colorful murals in towns across Nicaragua, which told the history of the revolution, have largely vanished from public view. The brush strokes of revolutionary artists are fast being covered over, many blackened out by Arnoldo Alemán, the former mayor of Managua and later president of Nicaragua (1997- ).

## The Demise of the FSLN

The electoral defeat of the Sandinista Party in 1990 sent shock waves around the world, and came as a surprise of immense proportions to supporters and politicians on both sides of the political divide. Daniel Ortega and the members of his National Directorate were stunned. They had always assumed a comfortable victory and were completely unprepared psychologically or practically for opposition. There was an urgent need for reflection, and party leaders and FSLN members gathered to analyze why they had lost the elections. The process of examining the reasons was exhaustive, and a long list of factors was identified. The nine years of war waged by the U.S. against Nicaragua and the tremendous human costs were an obvious part of any explanation of their defeat, but in the final analysis, the decline in the FSLN's popularity lay closer to home. The revolutionary leaders had grown apart from the people. They had simply failed to understand the nation's overwhelming desire for peace, whatever the political price.

More than anything else Nicaraguans wanted an end to the hardships brought by the Contra war. The Sandinista Party's promises of peace and prosperity rang hollow against the backdrop of a profound economic crisis and intensified Contra attacks. The war and the embargo were compounded by the Sandinistas' own economic mistakes, such as an initial weakness for large state-owned 'prestige projects' which in many cases turned into loss-making financial white elephants. Conscription was particularly unpopular, and as long as the draft was maintained, people found it difficult to believe that a peaceful resolution to the conflict was in sight. The FSLN

Ramirez and Ortega on the campaign trail together       *Julio Etchart/PANOS Pictures*

did consider abolishing conscription as a vote-winning device, but kept the electorate in suspense until the last rally of its election campaign. The thousands of supporters who packed Revolutionary Square and the surrounding streets of Managua, convinced the incumbent presidential candidate Ortega that he would win a decisive victory at the polls whatever policy he chose. On the basis of that enormous turn-out, the Sandinista Party decided to retain conscription.

### The Fall of an Icon

Throughout the years of the FSLN government up to the 1990 defeat, it was the energy and charisma of Ortega's leadership that held the country together. He was a skillful negotiator and a capable politician, but also a man of humble origins with whom the majority of poor Nicaraguans identified. His role in orchestrating the military defeat of the Somoza dictatorship made him a living legend. Ortega won the respect of intellectuals and peasants alike, but among the people to whom the revolution provided access to land, education and health services for the first time in their lives, he acquired cult status. Daniel, as he was affectionately known, was trusted. Huge crowds would flock to "Face the People" meetings in towns and villages across the country, where they listened attentively to his explanations of the nation's problems, asked questions and debated Sandinista policy. Many left those meetings more determined than ever to make whatever personal sacrifices they could for the revolution. His speeches were made clad in battle fatigues and using the colorful language of ordinary Nicaraguans; he understood how to communicate his commitment to the poor and disadvantaged.

The power of Nicaragua's president to motivate and inspire people did not suddenly disappear, but was quietly eroded by the daily struggle for survival. The improvements achieved in the early years of his government came to a halt, largely as a result of the war and the collapse of the country's economy. Although Ortega and his government were at pains to apportion the blame to the Contras and the U.S., their arguments could do little to prevent deteriorating living conditions and growing discontent. Benefits and privileges granted to FSLN officials, which included foreign travel, vehicles and access to luxury goods, caused increasing bitterness and resentment among some citizens. Rumors of extravagance were spread and the reported excesses of FSLN officials damaged the party's credibility.

Many Nicaraguans were cynical of the FSLN's double standards, but allegations of organized large-scale theft by the Sandinsta Party in the aftermath of the 1990 elections dramatically compounded the situation. Legislation known as "the piñata" was passed by the FSLN, guaranteeing the rights of people who had received land through the agrarian reform program, but also putting large amounts of state-owned properties into the hands of individuals. The leadership was accused of helping themselves to state assets as they prepared for opposition. A piñata is in fact a papier mâché animal stuffed with sweets which is broken open at children's parties; it was an image which sharply illustrated the perceived venality of Sandinista officials grasping the spoils of political office. The incident provoked a public outcry, fuelled by sensationalist reports in the rightwing press, which was quick to exploit the situation to the full. Although the FSLN conducted an internal investigation into the piñata, the extent of the corruption still remains largely unknown. The FSLN took action against some individual abuses, but the damage had been done, angering even some of the most loyal Sandinista supporters.

### The Sandinistas Divide

The FSLN was ill prepared for the criticism of its leadership, which its own members openly expressed. For the first time ever grievances were aired publicly. Sergio Ramirez, the former vice-president and an internationally respected author, was one of a growing group of Sandinistas calling for democratic reform. He articulated a widely shared concern about the lack of leadership accountability and internal democracy, arguing that the absence of genuine policy debate had frustrated activists and contributed to the decline in support for the FSLN. The centralization of power, which was necessary during the years of clandestine struggle against the Somoza dictatorship and the Contra war, he believed was no longer appropriate. Ortega's autocratic style had successfully dominated the politics of Nicaragua for almost a decade and was still deeply ingrained in the Sandinista Party. In new political circumstances his former strength had become a weakness, but Ortega and his followers were reluctant to admit the need for major change, and the process of democratizing the structures and procedures of the FSLN proved slow and problematic.

The compromise made by the FSLN leadership was to agree for the first time in its history to hold a party congress. The three-day assembly, which took place in July 1991, discussed the demands for greater political transparency and openness. The debate on a redefinition and modernization of the FSLN's program began, but was only the start of the party's deliberations, which continued right up until the 1996 election campaign. Two factions were evolving: the Democratic Left, which retained its commitment to a class-based struggle and was loyal to Ortega; and "Sandinismo for the Majority", which was influenced by social-democratic thought and grouped around Sergio Ramirez. In a second congress in May 1994, the party decided to elect and expand the membership of the National Directorate and the Sandinista Assembly. Quotas for women and young people were also introduced.

Ironically, the reforms worked against the modernizers. Sergio Ramirez was voted off the National Directorate by the Sandinista Assembly, an electoral college of the old party faithful. It also took the decision in September 1994 to remove him as the head of the Sandinista bench in the National Assembly. On the following day Ramirez announced his resignation from the party and the creation of the Sandinista Renovation Movement (MRS). He was joined by 32 of the 39 FSLN parliamentary deputies, as well as by a large number of high-profile professionals, artists and intellectuals, including Ernesto and Fernando Cardenal, priests who had been ministers in the former Sandinista government. There were bitter recriminations, personal attacks and even physical threats against people leaving the party. Carlos Fernando Chamorro, the editor of *Barricada*, the FSLN-owned newspaper, was sacked with the entirety of his staff because of their MRS sympathies. Although the MRS did not go on to win significant support at the polls, the split certainly further damaged the FSLN's credibility.

### Co-government

Differences in opinion on the FSLN's role in post-revolutionary Nicaragua sparked serious disagreements and divided the party. Ortega had declared his intention of using the impressive array of revolutionary organizations, which represented hundreds of thousands of people, as well as the FSLN's relatively strong position as the single largest party in the National Assembly, to defend the gains of the revolution. The policy, which Ortega described as "governing from below", was meant to apply pressure on the government through large-scale mobilizations of the trade unions and peasant movements on the streets. In practice though, the FSLN was wary of direct involvement in protests which threatened the country's fragile peace and damaged the economy. In the first year of Violeta Chamorro's administration, massive nation-wide demonstrations against her policies did take place, but they were organized independently of the FSLN, and only received the party's lukewarm support. The most radical Sandinistas were disappointed and accused the leadership of abandoning its commitment to the grassroots in favor of being co-opted by the government.

When Ortega participated in talks with UNO and decided to forge a more co-operative relationship with the government, he confirmed such fears. The FSLN wanted to help forge the conditions for peace and bring an end to the growing threat of civil war. National protests in May and July 1990 and transport strikes in 1993 and 1994 paralyzed the country and seriously risked an escalation of violence. In particular, the FSLN sought to avoid any association with the barricade-building and tire-burning activities of some protesters, who were widely blamed for deterring foreign investment and worsening the country's economic crisis. The party also condemned former Sandinista soldiers and Contras, who took up arms in the hope of forcing the government to meet their demands for land and improvements in living conditions. In trying to play a constructive role in opposition, Ortega did not appear to be doing enough to resist the hard-line economic policies of the UNO government, which resulted in a rapid increase in unemployment and poverty levels. In the end, the policy alienated many party members and brought few tangible rewards.

### Back to the Ballot Box

In the 1996 elections, the FSLN worked to project itself as a party of peace and moderation. It unveiled a manifesto that stressed the need for economic growth with social justice, foreign investment and the creation of jobs. In a controversial move which shocked many supporters, the party dropped its revolutionary anthem and replaced it with Beethoven's *Ode to Joy*. The FSLN's new look put Ortega in crisp white shirts, blue slacks and sensible shoes. On the campaign trail, he was always accompanied by his wife and children as the spin doctors worked hard to present him as a caring family man and to tone down the animated style of the former guerrilla leader.

But Ortega's passion for politics could not be repressed and he was invariably seen regaling the crowds from the roof of his jeep, waving his arms and punching the air with a clenched fist.

The image of the FSLN and the content of its election program had changed dramatically. The party machinery's tendency to direct proceedings remained, and the selection of its presidential and vice-presidential candidates was surrounded by controversy. For the first time, Ortega's nomination was challenged, and although he was declared the winning candidate, there were serious allegations of ballot-rigging. In the case of the vice-presidency, there were no elections at all and a candidate unknown to party members – José Manuel Caldera, a wealthy rancher and member of COSEP, the right-wing Private Enterprise Council – was imposed by the leadership. The appointment of Caldera, a self-confessed non-Sandinista, was justified as a move to broaden support for the FSLN, which was running its election campaign under the slogan "Nicaragua for Everyone", and to enhance its credibility as a modern democratic party, capable of forming a government of national unity.

The electorate remained unconvinced of the FSLN's suitability for government and it lost the 1996 elections. Two consecutive defeats at the ballot box and internal rifts have severely weakened the Sandinista Party. Ortega has clung to his position as party leader, but under his stewardship the FSLN's attempt to project a new image and revive its political fortunes have been largely unsuccessful. Although he has survived challenges and attacks, the party has been unable to unite behind him. The chances of Ortega winning the nomination as presidential candidate for elections in 2001 have no doubt been further reduced by damaging allegations against him of sexual abuse by his step-daughter, Zoilamérica Narváez. In March 1998, she spoke publicly about her alleged ordeal of repeated sexual abuse since the age of eleven. Her allegations rocked the political community and opened still more divisions within the Sandinista Party. Daniel Ortega has used his parliamentary immunity to prevent the case being brought to court.

### The Chamorro Presidency

If the recent period of Daniel Ortega's leadership has been plagued by accusations of abuse, the personal reputation of his former political adversary in the 1990 election has remained squeaky clean. It is an irony of Nicaraguan politics that the once charismatic and forceful leader of the revolution was upstaged by a grandmother. Violeta Chamorro, the widow of Pedro Joaquín Chamorro and UNO's presidential candidate, was widely dismissed as a frail figure, lacking in political experience and subservient to her U.S. paymaster. As the matriarch of a politically divided family and

Daniel Ortega congratulates
Violeta Chamorro on her election win

*Reuters*

a devout Catholic, however, she struck a chord with voters and a played an important role in UNO's electoral victory.

The appointment of Chamorro as UNO's presidential candidate was the result of a compromise between fourteen diverse political parties, an alliance brought together under the aegis of the U.S. just months before the 1990 elections. It was made up of liberals, conservatives, social democrats and even communists, groups with almost nothing in common apart from an interest in the generous funding on offer and getting the Sandinista Party out of power. The process of selecting the coalition's candidates was extremely difficult and almost broke it apart. The only way forward was to share power between the various factions. Chamorro's image as a moderate, without any political affiliation, provided an acceptable counterbalance to the vice-presidential candidate, Virgilio Godoy, an ardent anti-Sandinista and the leader of one of the right-wing liberal parties.

UNO's election campaign was lacking in substance and poorly organized. Although some of its member parties got out among the electorate and made a serious attempt to win votes, others simply sat back in anticipation of the FSLN landslide predicted by the opinion polls. The task of projecting an anti-Sandinista message was more effectively carried out by the right-wing forces of the national newspaper *La Prensa*, COSEP and Cardinal Obando y Bravo, the head of the Roman Catholic Church. In contrast, UNO's friendship with the U.S. was championed as guaranteed to end the Contra war and to boost the economy. Any doubt in voters' minds was erased by a statement from U.S. President Bush, promising to the lift the economic embargo against Nicaragua if the Sandinistas were defeated at the ballot box.

### An Uneasy Alliance

When UNO won the elections, there were widespread fears of an outbreak of fighting between the defeated Sandinistas and the Contras. In order to diffuse the threat of civil war, Chamorro showed herself as a far shrewder politician than expected by turning to an unexpected source of support: the defeated Sandinista Party. Her son-in-law Antonio Lacayo, for whom she created the position of Minister of the Presidency, held secret discussions with the FSLN on a Transition Protocol, an agreement aimed at ensuring a peaceful hand-over of power. In the document signed on April 25, 1990, the Sandinistas won some major concessions. Most significantly, the Sandinista-created army was left largely intact. It would, however, be de-politicized, bringing an end to the joint holding of political and military office. It was also dramatically reduced in size from 82,000 to 41,000 members. In an extremely controversial decision, Chamorro agreed to retain Humberto Ortega, Daniel Ortega's brother, as the head of the army. The right wing and the U.S. were outraged, and it remained an issue of contention until his eventual removal in 1995.

### Collapse of UNO

Once in power, the UNO coalition began to unravel. The right-wing parties, under the leadership of Vice-President Virgilio Godoy, unleashed a campaign for the removal of Chamorro. Godoy promised to deliver the destruction of the Sandinista revolution and to clear its supporters from every last tier of government. Although Chamorro served out her term as president, she had limited support within the National Assembly, where only the center parties of UNO remained loyal. In order to govern effectively she was forced to make deals with the FSLN, which usually co-operated in order to contain the influence of right-wing extremists. She also frequently resorted to the use of presidential decrees, a feature of government that was widely criticized as undemocratic and eventually abolished as part of constitutional reforms.

With the loyalty of the army and police guaranteed by the Transition Protocol, Chamorro was able to move the peace process forward. Plans were drawn up to resettle the Contras and considerable investment, in areas known as *polos de desarrollo* or "development poles", was prom-ised to ease their integration into civil society. The UNO government also granted the ex-insurgents representation in government ministries and allowed them to form their own security forces to patrol the development poles. And although the armed activities of Contra malcontents contin-ued, President Chamorro declared the war over on June 27, 1990.

On the economic front, the UNO government wasted no time in draw-ing up plans to reduce the country's budget deficit and restore productivity. World Bank-style stabilization and structural adjustment measures were introduced almost immediately. In the early years of the Chamorro administration, the trade union movement successfully mobilized people against drastic cuts in public expenditure. In response to a series of nationwide strikes, the UNO government adopted a strategy of negotiation. Through a dialogue with workers and employers known as the *concertación*, UNO managed to reduce social tensions and push ahead with its economic reform program. Although it found less confrontational ways of implementing its policies, they still brought massive unemployment and a sharp decline in living standards. By the end of Chamorro's six-year term in 1996, the market economy was well established.

### Nicaragua's Strongman: Arnoldo Alemán

Billboards set at regular intervals along the busiest streets of Managua tell people that the "Mayor gets things done". They refer to the superficial changes made to the capital by Arnoldo Alemán, the former mayor of Managua. And even as president, he remained proud of the heavily guarded shopping malls, the gas stations and fast food outlets built during his five years in the town hall. But the trappings of a modern capital are a mirage. The desperate poverty which characterizes the real Managua is never far away. Flimsy shacks flank the road leading from the Inter-Continental Hotel to Lake Managua, which Alemán lined with fountains and palms for the visit of King Juan Carlos of Spain in 1992. Groups of small children beg on the steps of Pizza Hut and prostitutes wait on a newly built roundabout, a short walk from Managua's modern cathedral.

Alemán comes from a farming family which supported the Somoza dictatorship in the hills of El Crucero. He spent most of the first year after the 1979 revolution in prison, and his property along with the estates of other associates of the old regime was confiscated by the Sandinista government. Despite Alemán's strong contempt for the revolution, he remained in Nicaragua throughout the 1980s, working as a lawyer and expanding his profitable coffee interests. He came to prominence as the mayor of Managua in 1990 and began to build his political empire, frequently coming into conflict with the FSLN, which accused him of corruption. A long drawn-out court case eventually found a number of the mayor's officials guilty of pocketing public funds, but their misdemeanors did not damage Alemán's popularity.

The country's rich élite was Alemán's natural constituency, as it shared his hatred of the revolution and its leaders. He also attracted a following among the inhabitants of the sprawling slums of Managua, who were impressed by the veneer of the city's modernization. Although they could never afford to see the American movies showing in large air-conditioned cinemas or benefit from the drive-in restaurants, the developments inspired hope and won their support. As the presidential candidate for the Liberal Alliance, a coalition of four right-wing parties, Alemán built on the mass appeal of U.S. culture. On the campaign trail he talked of the need for modernization and large-scale foreign investment, which he argued the Liberal Alliance was best placed to deliver. One of its slogans was "War on Unemployment and Misery" and Alemán appeared to promise that the poorest and most marginalized sectors would be part of ambitious economic plans to take the country into the twenty-first century.

From the opening of the electoral contest in August 1996, the Liberal Alliance was permanently on the road. Alemán traveled in a convoy of four-wheel drives, carrying a team of U.S.-trained campaign organizers and a vast assortment of paraphernalia for distribution at rallies. It was an efficient and precise operation, covering the length and breadth of the country. Funds to pay for the campaign poured in from wealthy Nicaraguans and the powerful anti-Castro lobby living in the U.S. It was an investment which they expected to deliver returns once Alemán was installed as president.

Nicaragua wanted a strong leader to take over from Chamorro, and the electorate duly gave Alemán the job. The Liberal Alliance declared itself victorious in the early hours of October 21, 1996, although the official result was not announced by the Supreme Electoral Council for another month, due to an investigation into claims of fraud. Although irregularities, including the discovery of ballot papers in the possession of Liberal Alliance officials were brought to light, the size of the vote for Alemán ensured that the overall result remained unchanged. In the final count the Liberal Alliance secured 52 percent and the FSLN 38 percent.

Since Alemán's inauguration in January 1997 an uneasy tension has existed between his populist rhetoric and the actions of his government. As yet, the ambitious campaign promises of the Liberal Alliance remain largely unfulfilled. The key policy aim of creating the conditions for economic recovery has taken priority over securing an increase in employment and the standard of living for the poor majority of citizens. And even here there has been only limited success. The stability of the country, which the government has sought as a precondition for foreign investment, continues to be damaged by the violence of armed bands in the countryside, for whom there is little incentive to lay down their weapons.

The strikes and demonstrations which so undermined the Chamorro administration have not caused Alemán as many problems. In particular, the power of the trade union movement has been reduced, weakened by contractions in the workforce, fear of redundancy and internal divisions. The wave of repression, which opponents of the Liberal Alliance feared, has not materialized in the form anticipated. Although there were serious disputes with the country's large number of non-governmental organizations (NGOs) and the women's movement in the first few months, Alemán's government has since adopted a less confrontational style and introduced its highly patriarchal and morally conservative agenda gradually.

On the campaign trail, the Alemán government talked of taking a tough stance in negotiations with the international financial institutions. In reality, agreements with the IMF and World Bank, which were renewed in 1998, merely reinforced the economic reforms undertaken by the Chamorro administration. The succession of two neo-liberal administrations has transformed Nicaragua beyond recognition. Their support for radical economic reforms has pushed a growing number of people below the poverty line and into unemployment. An estimated 75 percent of the population are now unable to adequately feed or clothe themselves and 60 percent are out of work. Cuts in spending on health and education, the removal of food subsidies and the loss of agricultural credit have combined to worsen the situation of the majority. In an attempt to make ends meet, women, men and children have taken to the streets, where they sell any assortment of goods. The competition is fierce and the returns minuscule. In desperation, others have turned to crime and prostitution, which are invariably more lucrative. Before 1990, Managua was safe to wander in, but it is now becoming increasingly dangerous and attacks on foreigners have become commonplace. Gangs with knives and AK-47s have sprung up, often associated with the capital's recently established role in the drugs trade.

### Rolling Back Land Reform

A bulldozer crashes through a field of bananas in La Cumplida, the site of what was once a state farm in the mountainous department of Matagalpa. The former owner, whose property was confiscated by the Sandinista government, is attempting to drive the peasants farming the land away. He has already intimidated some into selling their plots cheaply, but others refuse to surrender their livelihood so easily. They will wait for the courts to examine the case, but in the meantime they will need to fight to keep possession of their property.

In the 1980s the Sandinista government undertook a series of land reforms to reverse the grossly unequal patterns of ownership under the Somoza dictatorship. These measures benefited an estimated 200,000 peasant families, who worked their own land for the first time. After the defeat of the FSLN in 1990, their situation looked increasingly insecure. Thousands of former owners, many arriving back from the U.S., demanded the return of their properties. Alejandro Somoza, a nephew of the dictator,

Small farmers receive land titles from the Sandinista government, 1984    *Jenny Matthews/Network*

filed claims for over 50 family properties valued at $250 million. Although the UNO government was bound by the Transition Protocol, the agreement signed with the FSLN to leave the revolutionary reforms untouched, a presidential decree authorized a review of confiscations. The initiative signaled the start of a politically complex dispute that has fuelled outbreaks of violence and contributed to the country's instability.

The arduous process of examining an estimated 5,500 claims began in 1991, but in the absence of documentation made limited headway. Determining whether the properties belonged to the claimants or were foreclosed rather than confiscated caused delays. While bureaucrats poured over bank records, some people resorted to force, hiring armed gangs to evict families from land they considered their own. Tensions escalated as a result of violent repossessions and the UNO government's failure to uphold the law. Unions representing peasants and small farmers organized a network of local committees and attempted, with varying degrees of success, to prevent former owners from seizing land illegally.

It took the intervention of right-wing U.S. senators on behalf of Nicaraguans who had become American citizens to persuade Violeta Chamorro to take more decisive action. The pressure they exerted culminated in the threat of applying the Helms-Burton legislation, which allows for aid to be withheld from countries where the property of U.S. citizens has been confiscated. Fearing the suspension of U.S. funds and the blocking of multilateral loans, the Chamorro administration reached an agreement which became the 1995 Property Stability Law. The Confiscation Association, which was formed to campaign for the return of properties, was opposed to the terms of the settlement and forced Alemán to re-open the issue.

President Alemán had promised the wholesale return of confiscated property, but abandoned his election pledge in the face of fierce grassroots protests. He opted for a solution acceptable to the Sandinista Party, which became law in November 1997. Former owners of urban plots of less than 100 square meters and rural property of less than 35 hectares would be compensated and the estimated 100,000 beneficiaries of the Sandinista agrarian reforms would receive long-awaited titles to the land. Individuals, including many high-ranking FSLN officials occupying larger holdings, would be expected to pay or return their assets. The Confiscation Association has pledged to fight on, outraged by the government's refusal to reverse the reforms in their entirety and what it regards as inadequate arrangements for compensation.

## Democracy and Elections

Nicaraguans are passionately interested in politics. Loud and animated debate on current affairs can often be overheard in markets, buses and on street corners. Yet only a very small number of people are formally affiliated to political parties, with the exception of the Sandinista Party, which in 1995 had a membership of over 300,000. The legal requirements for setting up political parties are minimal, but despite the efforts of scores of newcomers, the Nicaraguan electorate has not been persuaded to abandon its loyalties to either the FSLN or the long-established Liberal and Conservative parties. 24 parties and alliances registered to participate in the 1996 elections, but only five secured more than one representative in the National Assembly.

Although there is some evidence of a growing cynicism towards politicians and their grandiose promises, it has not yet kept people away from the polling booths. The right to vote is still regarded as an important feature of Nicaragua's fledgling democracy. The turn-out in the 1996 elections was very high, with two million people or over 80 percent of the electorate voting. This was despite a bizarrely complicated procedure which involved marking six ballot papers to elect the president, vice-president, 90 National Assembly deputies, 20 representatives of the Central American Parliament and the mayors and vice-mayors of the country's 145 municipalities. The ballot papers were printed with a confusing array of 24 party logos and were almost six feet long. They rarely fitted on the tables provided at polling stations, and tested the patience of voters as they struggled to find the party of their choice. It was a time-consuming process, but people waited their turn, often standing for hours in the burning sun.

Elections have been held in Nicaragua for over 150 years, but until the overthrow of the Somoza dictatorship, they were no more than a rubber stamping of agreements between the country's ruling families. The first genuine elections were held in 1984 and were comfortably won by the ruling Sandinistas, and although the process was derided by the U.S. as fraudulent, international observers declared the vote free and fair. When voters returned to the polls in 1990, however, they opted for a center-right coalition, and in 1996 Nicaragua appeared to complete the circle politically by voting for the Liberal Alliance, a group of parties with links to the former Somoza dictatorship. If the pollsters are to be believed, the elections due to be held in 2001 will be a two-horse race between the Liberal Alliance and the FSLN.

### Civil Society and Non-Governmental Organizations (NGOs)

The commitment of Nicaragua's citizens to the democratic process extends well beyond the cycle of elections. Hundreds of thousands of ordinary people are involved in a myriad of groups, organizations and campaigns, which are working to improve their lives.

A walk through almost any town in Nicaragua will probably take you past the offices of projects for the rural poor, demobilized soldiers, people with disabilities or street children. A large number of international organizations involved in emergency aid or longer-term development projects have a strong presence. There are also over 300 domestic non-governmental organizations (NGOs), the majority of which were set up in the aftermath of the FSLN electoral defeat in 1990. Many were formed by Sandinistas, who anticipated a dramatic erosion of the revolution's social achievements and began to work with the country's poorest and most disadvantaged citizens. The combined forces of the non-governmental sector now play an extremely important role in meeting people's basic needs and in lobbying the government to invest in human development. Yet despite the proliferation of development organizations, they are powerless to fill the fast growing gaps in services previously provided by the state.

The vast operations of the UN agencies, the U.S. Agency for International Development and the European Union, or even the more modest programs of Nicaraguan NGOs, often overshadow the hundreds of grassroots self-help projects. These initiatives are run by local people, often with the support of foreign solidarity organizations or twin town links. They are the legacy of an impressive international solidarity movement for Nicaragua, inspired by the 1979 revolution. Thousands of people from North America, Latin America and Europe joined delegations and study tours to learn about the country at first hand. An impressive array of ce-

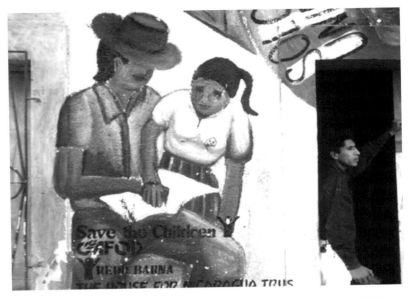

Mural, showing NGO names, Estelí                    *Jon Spaull/PANOS Pictures*

lebrities sympathetic to the revolution were also welcomed by the Sandinista government. International brigades helped bring in the coffee harvest, a contribution which was more about showing solidarity with Nicaraguans than the returns on the sacks of beans they brought down from steep mountain slopes. Support groups, although reduced in number, are still fundraising for projects, organizing brigades and campaigning on behalf of poor Nicaraguans.

The size and influence of Nicaragua's NGO sector and solidarity movement is difficult to measure, but it still brings significant funds into the country. Indeed, the Liberal Alliance considered the income worthy of tighter controls and in 1997 proposed amending the law regulating domestic NGOs. It failed to take into account the political clout of the development sector's international links. The enormous outcry extended beyond Nicaragua as foreign donors, large and small, rushed to protect the autonomy of their partner organizations. President Alemán was forced to withdraw the proposed changes and tolerate the operations of NGOs, many of which have their origins in the Sandinista revolution.

### The Women's Movement

A flurry of research reports recently published about violence against women makes shocking reading. They show that more than half of Nicaraguan women have experienced physical, psychological or sexual abuse at the hands of their husbands or boyfriends. It is therefore no wonder that a series of national campaigns against male violence have galvanised enormous interest and helped set up some innovative support structures. One is the creation of a network of women's police stations, which aims to encourage women to register complaints and take legal action against their partners. Specially trained police women run the units and work closely with local women's organisations to provide advice and counselling services. As a result fewer women are dropping their cases and the number of convictions against violent men has increased. There are also projects training women to speak out and stand up to violence in the family, which traditionally they have been expected to tolerate.

Nicaragua is a profoundly patriarchal society, in which women are widely considered subordinate to men. The struggle to promote sexual equality and opportunity began with the 1979 revolution, but the development of a feminist movement, arguing for fundamental changes in the relationship between women and men, is a more recent phenomenon. Under the Sandinista government, the situation of women advanced dramatically as a result of access to education, health services and improvements in living conditions. However, the culture of *machismo*, which kept women in their roles of mothers and carers, was largely unchanged. The Luisa Amanda Espinosa Association of Nicaraguan Women (AMNLAE) helped push forward important advances, but ultimately was more concerned with involving women in the revolutionary process than challenging unequal power relations between men and women.

In the 1990s the ideas of feminists, who had been largely sidelined within the FSLN, came to prominence and helped create a vibrant and diverse women's movement. A wide variety of initiatives has been established by urban and rural women, intellectuals and professionals. They are not formally organized as a network, but loose co-ordination exists which enables the women's movement to come together when necessary. Such situations have arisen since Alemán came to power, as the influence of reactionary forces, in particular the conservative sectors of the Catholic Church, has grown. Cardinal Obando y Bravo and Humberto Belli, the former Minister of Education, have led a moral crusade against sex outside of marriage, family planning and abortion. They have already succeeded in dismantling the Institute for Women, which was set up to promote women's rights, and have replaced it with the Ministry of the Family. Despite a campaign that mobilized widespread national and international support, the Liberal Alliance pushed ahead with its plan, waiting until the uproar had died down before taking the bill introducing the changes through the National Assembly.

Teachers on strike, Managua                    *Tony Morrison/South American Pictures*

While the women's movement has established itself effectively from the grassroots up, its links with formal politics are weak. None of the few women who have held powerful political positions has advocated equality, including Violeta Chamorro, Nicaragua's first woman president. Attempts to increase women's representation through a cross-party initiative in the 1996 elections ended in failure and the number of women at all levels of government fell. Only ten women won seats in the National Assembly, eight of whom belong to the FSLN. None of the incumbents wields any special influence through appointments to ministries or commissions.

### Mixed Fortunes: The Trade Union Movement

It is one of the contradictions of the developing world that drinking water is often hard to get hold of, but alcoholic and soft beverages always seem to be in abundant supply. In Nicaragua, crates of Victoria beer and Pepsi reach the remotest corners of the country. Multinationals are usually making the profits, but surprisingly in the case of Victoria and Pepsi, a small number of workers have shared in the financial rewards. Since the privatization of state farms and industries began in 1990, a wide range of worker-owned companies have gone into business with varying degrees of success. There is a meat-processing plant in Managua, a soap factory in Granada, tobacco and cigar makers in Estelí and a leather workshop in Condega.

The phenomenon of worker-ownership is the result of a complex and risky negotiation process with the UNO government, but also a reflection of the influence once wielded by the country's powerful trade unions. During the 1980s workers were actively encouraged to organize and their leaders enjoyed a positive relationship with the Sandinista government. When political circumstances changed in 1990, the majority of the workforce in formal employment was unionized and prepared to oppose the Chamorro administration's plans to privatize state farms and industries. A wave of strikes and protests brought the country to a halt and persuaded the UNO government of the need to negotiate with the trade unions.

The UNO government opened negotiations with the two largest trades unions, the Association of Rural Workers (ATC) and the Industrial Workers' Union (CST), which otherwise threatened to prevent the implementation of its privatization program. In an extremely controversial move, the trade union leaders decided to accept a 25 percent stake in state companies. In order to secure outright control over some companies, they agreed to receive up to 100 percent of shares in some and none in others. The majority of workers were entirely excluded from the benefits of the agreement, and left without any guarantees as to their employment prospects in the private sector. Tensions built up as their leaders increasingly dedicated themselves to their new roles as managers of the worker-owned companies. The policy proved extremely divisive and marked the beginning of a dramatic decline in the influence of the ATC and CST.

The privatization process has massively weakened the trade union movement. Large-scale lay-offs and cuts in public sector spending have been particularly damaging. Nevertheless FETSALUD, the health workers' union and ANDEN, the teachers' union, are examples of organizations which have redoubled their efforts to motivate activists and improve the capacity of their members to deal with violations of labor law and the deterioration of work conditions. They have also had some success in renegotiating collective bargaining agreements with the government, which provides their members with some job security. In a long-standing dispute, doctors even won themselves a pay rise in mid-1998 and are supporting the FETSALUD campaign against the introduction of charges in the health service. While the trade union movement is unlikely ever to recapture the power and influence it enjoyed in the 1980s, some workers' organizations will continue to play an important role in the country's politics.

# 3    ECONOMY: IN SEARCH OF RECOVERY

Clusters of people make their way up to the coffee slopes of Matagalpa in northern Nicaragua. The sun is beginning to break through the low-lying morning mist and they waste no time in getting down to work. Nimble hands move up and down the branches of shoulder-high bushes, dropping the plump red berries into baskets tied around their waists. The coffee harvest is a labor-intensive operation and between November and January provides tens of thousands of men, women and children with employment. Usually paid by weight, a moderately fast picker can earn up to $2.50 a day. People and sometimes entire communities arrive from all parts of the country to take part in this seasonal migration, often travelling large distances for the wages on which they attempt to survive for the remaining months of the year.

## A Rural Economy

Just a handful of crops dominates the Nicaraguan economy. Coffee is the most important and has held its position as its most valuable export for more than a century. But it is a business fraught with difficulties. A drop in the price on the world market or early rains, causing the beans to rot on the bushes and wiping out the whole crop, can spell economic disaster, such is the country's reliance on coffee sales. The prices of other key agricultural products, including sugarcane, bananas and meat also suffer from the vagaries of the international market and weather. Yet despite the inherent problems of cash crops, farming is the mainstay of Nicaragua's economy. It provides almost a third of the country's foreign earnings and is a vital source of employment. Almost half of the population of 4.4 million still live in the countryside, working as wage laborers on large farms or growing their own food on small plots of land.

The challenge of strengthening the agricultural export sector has tested policy-makers throughout successive administrations, but boom and bust cycles continue. International demand is difficult to predict, with climate changes, technological advances and the tastes of first-world consumers all playing their part. The fate of the cotton industry, once Nicaragua's second largest export, is a telling example. Until the 1980s, large land-owners on the western plains of León and Chinandega made huge profits from cotton. But production was only sustained by the application of increasing concentrations of highly toxic pesticides, which pushed up the production costs. In the meantime the international market became ever

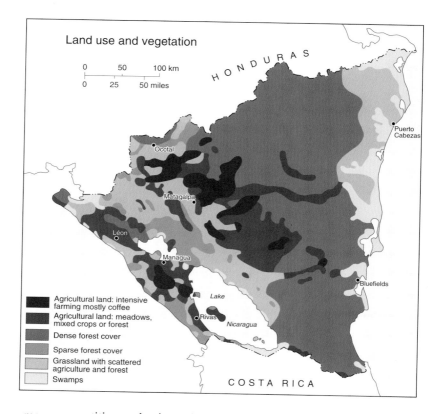

Land use and vegetation

0    50    100 km
0    25    50 miles

HONDURAS

Ocotal

Matagalpa

Léon

Managua

Puerto Cabezas

Bluefields

Lake

Rivas

Nicaragua

■ Agricultural land: intensive farming mostly coffee
■ Agricultural land: meadows, mixed crops or forest
■ Dense forest cover
■ Sparse forest cover
■ Grassland with scattered agriculture and forest
■ Swamps

COSTA RICA

more competitive and prices plummeted. The industry had collapsed by the late 1980s and the snowy white fields gave way to vast expanses of idle land which is now barren and unfit for cultivation.

The rapid expansion of exports such as cotton has exacted a high human and environmental price. The excessive use of chemicals, many of which are banned in the industrialized world, has poisoned workers, reduced the fertility of the land and contaminated the country's rivers. The production of basic grains, which feeds the population, has also fallen sharply as land, agricultural credit and investment are increasingly geared to serve the international market. Even the Sandinista government, which aimed to make the country self-sufficient in food, was unable to end its dependency on imports. Nicaragua, considered the granary of Central America in the 1960s, now makes regular purchases of wheat and rice and receives large amounts of food aid from Europe and North America.

Politics has had a lot to do with the fate of agricultural production. The 1979 revolution resulted in changes in Nicaragua's trading partners. The

U.S. trade embargo introduced in 1985 closed long established markets, which had accounted for a substantial proportion of exports. New buyers in Europe, Asia and the former Eastern bloc were eventually found, but the shift disrupted the sales of some products. The sugar growers suffered massive losses, and although production in the northwest still survives, the industry has never fully recovered. The growth of the banana trade was also held back in the 1980s, limited by the costs of transporting the fragile fruit further to new markets. Nicaragua has also had to deal with stiff competition from neighboring Central American countries, where U.S. companies invested heavily in large-scale production.

## Economic Crisis

Nicaragua has faced serious economic problems since the late 1970s when earnings from agriculture began to decline. They fell even more steeply with the onset of the Contra war and the U.S. embargo in the mid-1980s. Exports dropped by more than half and foreign exchange shortages severely restricted imports vital to agricultural production. The cost of living rose and inflation ran wild, reaching over 36,000 percent in 1988. The government printed money at a furious rate and, in a desperate attempt to keep up with inflation, even added a string of zeros to bank notes in circulation. People rushed to cash their pay checks as quickly as possible, but the value of their wages decreased even as they stood in line at the bank.

The crisis required urgent action, and the measures that the FSLN was forced to take marked the beginning of Nicaragua's "structural adjustment", a painful process of restricting expenditure to match income. In similar circumstances in other developing countries, the International Monetary Fund and the World Bank would arrive to impose public-sector cuts and to create the conditions for free trade, in return for the external financing in the form of loans to ease the transition. But in Nicaragua, the Sandinista government was forced to experiment with the implementation of hard-hitting measures without the assistance of foreign aid.

In 1988, with the aim of bringing inflation under control and encouraging exports, a massive monetary reform was undertaken. In a spectacular operation, during which the borders were sealed for three days, a new currency was issued to an unsuspecting public. Illegal money changers, who had wreaked havoc with the economy, offering as much as ten times the official rate for American dollars, temporarily went out of business. Daniel Ortega adopted a somber tone and appeared on the government's television channels and radio stations to explain and reassure the public of the pressing need for austerity. The new currency was followed by increases in utility prices, restrictions on credit and cuts in government spending. The measures failed to stabilize the economy, largely due to the continuing costs of the Contra war and the costs of repairing extensive damage caused by a hurricane, which swept through Nicaragua in 1988.

## Debt

Every government since the Somoza dictatorship has been forced to borrow abroad. In 1979 an inherited debt of $1.6 billion obliged the Sandinista government to borrow to rebuild the country and underwrite its investments in education, health services and agriculture. Loans and aid, largely from the former Eastern bloc countries, kept the economy afloat, but interest payments were suspended and the debt grew rapidly. By 1994 the accumulation of interest on old and new debt brought the total amount owed to foreign governments, banks and institutions to a staggering $11 billion. In per capita terms each woman, man and child owed approximately $3,000 to external creditors, the highest per capita debt in the world. It was an impossible situation: Nicaragua could not even afford to meet its interest payments, which were larger than the entirety of its annual export earnings, let alone pay off the debt.

Nicaragua, along with numerous other developing countries caught in the vicious circle of growing indebtedness, was faced with no other option than compliance with IMF and World Bank policies of stabilization and structural adjustment. Both the UNO and Liberal Alliance governments have consequently been required to resume debt payments, but they have also benefited from a series of debt cancellation agreements. Individual creditors including Russia and Mexico, the Paris Club (a group of the wealthiest industrialized countries), and some commercial banks wrote off large amounts of Nicaragua's debt, which was reduced to $6.3 billion by 1998. Yet despite the halving of the debt, repayments are still unmanageable and the campaign for further debt relief continues.

## Under IMF Tutelage

A full-fledged stabilization and structural adjustment program began in 1990. The UNO government, proclaiming its allegiance to the free market ethic, embarked on a course of public spending reduction, liberalization and privatization. In a preparatory stage, Nicaragua worked to comply with IMF loan conditions to qualify for money that was desperately needed to help make the difficult transition to the market economy. The country qualified in 1991 for new loans from the international financial institutions after it cleared its debt service arrears to the multilateral financial institutions such as the World Bank and the IMF and promised to resume regular repayments.

Enormous amounts of foreign finance were consequently released to prop up the economy, but were strictly conditional on the implementation of the country's economic plan. Between 1990 and 1995 Nicaragua received a total of $3.2 billion from foreign governments and international financial institutions. In reality, however, it only received a small proportion of the paper figure as most contributions were earmarked for repayments on the national debt. The anticipated level of aid from the U.S. did not materialize and was disbursed slowly in an attempt to influence political changes, in particular the resolution of the property dispute. Of $300 million committed to the first year of Violeta Chamorro's term in office, only $160 million was ever paid.

### Public Expenditure Cuts

No time was wasted in cutting back on the apparatus and services of the state. Health workers, teachers, the police and the army were laid off in growing numbers. By 1993 public expenditure was squeezed to 27 percent of Gross Domestic Product (GDP), compared to the record 59 percent of GDP spent by the FSLN in 1984. The cuts provoked a strong reaction from the trade union movement, which took to the streets in May and July 1990, effectively bringing the country to a standstill. The UNO government was cautious about cracking down on the demonstrations, as it believed repression would harden the protesters' resolve and deepen the conflict. A minimum level of social stability was required if UNO was to bring about an economic recovery, and in order to achieve that it was prepared to compromise.

In a process known as the *concertación*, the government, trade unions and employers participated in talks to reach agreements acceptable to all sides. UNO suspended its cutbacks in the public sector, but introduced what it euphemistically described as a "job conversion program". Over 22, 000 people were enticed into voluntary retirement by one-off payments of about $2,000 made by the U.S. Agency for International Development, which were intended to help in setting up small businesses. Most were unsuccessful and many participants in the scheme became unemployed. Meanwhile, the UNO government made big savings on its public-sector wage bill and succeeded in avoiding a head-on conflict with the trade union movement.

### Extended Structural Adjustment Fund (ESAF)

In keeping with the times, protesters in Nicaragua nowadays unfurl banners saying "ESAF kills" or "Adjustment costs lives". They are all too aware of the role of the IMF and the World Bank in the country's rising poverty and unemployment, and are almost as familiar with the workings of the international financial institutions as with those of their own government.

Anti telephone privatization graffiti                    *Jon Spaull/PANOS Pictures*

The first Extended Structural Adjustment Fund (ESAF) agreement was signed between the IMF and the Nicaraguan government in April 1994. It committed the country to a package of extensive reforms and set targets against which loans would be released. The UNO government made patchy progress on the reforms, and despite renegotiating its targets, the IMF suspended funds in September 1996. ESAF I expired in 1997 and it was not until March 1998 that the Liberal Alliance finally reached agreement on ESAF II. It outlined new commitments to cutting social spending and increases in the price of the public utilities, which if ever implemented, will prove highly unpopular.

### Privatization

Privatization has been a central tenet of the ESAF agreements. The UNO government prioritized the return into private hands of banks, industry and farms nationalized by the FSLN in the 1980s. However, laying the ground for the sale of profitable enterprises and the liquidation of loss-making companies was a slow and complex process. Opposition from the 78,000 employees of the 351 state-owned companies forced the Chamorro administration into negotiations with their unions. Eventually a deal was reached, which made a small minority of workers into shareholders and cleared the way for an extensive privatization program.

The state banks were also a key target for privatization, although they were protected by the Constitution. Undeterred, the UNO government exploited a legal loophole, which allowed private banks to enter the market, which they now dominate. Meanwhile, Chamorro restricted the activities of the state banks, made staff cuts and closed a large number of branches. Other institutions on the list for privatization included ENITEL, the country's telecommunications company. But a hard-fought trade union campaign and bitter argument in the National Assembly delayed the sale of a 40 percent stake in the profit-making business. With the approval of legislation for its privatization in June 1998, the process has moved ahead and is time-tabled for completion by the end of 1999.

### Rising Cost of Living

A private pharmacy, selling a bewildering array of drugs and medical equipment, is never more than a few blocks away in Nicaragua. The spread of all-purpose medical outlets throughout its towns and villages is symbolic of the decline of the country's health service. Patients were previously treated for free, but they are now charged. Instead of medicines, they are issued prescriptions, the costs of which few can afford. Pills and tablets, even antibiotics, are consequently sold individually to suit the customers' purse rather than their need.

The impact of economic reform, in particular large cuts in per capita spending on health care and education, has been catastrophic. The poorest sectors of society, already struggling to meet their basic food needs, are now rarely able to find the money to pay for hospital visits, medicines or school fees. The elimination of subsidies and the removal of price controls have simply pushed the cost of living beyond the means of the majority of the population. In a study carried out in 1995 by NITLAPAN, an independent economic research institute, 36.6 percent of the urban population was categorized as "severely impoverished" and a further 30 percent as "poor".

The situation in rural Nicaragua is even worse. In 1995 the World Bank estimated that 75 percent of people in the countryside lived in poverty. A growing number, in particular children, are malnourished. Economic policies and failed harvests are largely responsible. Many subsistence and small farmers can no longer afford seeds or tools to work their land. Credit for domestic production has more or less dried up as the banks tighten their control over the money supply in response to IMF requirements. In addition, massive reductions in import tariffs have opened the domestic market to an influx of cheaper produce from neighboring countries, which has put some local producers out of business. The results are devastating and threaten to accelerate migration to the towns, where the prospects of survival are little better.

## Export-Led Growth

The painful belt-tightening measures geared to reactivating the economy have failed to improve the lot of the majority of Nicaraguans. Yet the wealthiest members of the business community have benefited enormously and taken advantage of incentives to increase the country's foreign exchange earnings. With the approval of the international financial institutions, they have received credit to modernize and expand their enterprises. Sales of coffee, sugar, meat and bananas have improved, as well as newly-established exports of seafood, sesame, melons and onions. Revenues from tourism, timber, mining and garment-assembly have made a particularly strong showing. And in 1995 the country recorded a five percent increase in its GDP for the first time in ten years. Foreign investment in agricultural production, manufacturing and the country's infrastructure has also helped to boost output.

The growth of traditional and alternative agriculture was seriously hampered by the difficulties and expense of transporting produce across and out of the country, even before Hurricane Mitch destroyed large parts of the infrastructure. The situation is now even more problematic, and investment in rebuilding roads and bridges is urgently needed. Until access to rural areas, which are poorly connected by dirt tracks to a small network of surfaced roads and the Pan-American Highway, is improved, farmers will struggle to secure stable markets for their crops. The limited capacity of the country's six seaports on the Pacific and Atlantic coasts also frustrates the movement of goods. Corinto is currently the most suitable port for commercial shipping, and investment in the expansion of its facilities is planned. In the meantime, most produce travels by road to ports in Costa Rica and Honduras. A faster, but more expensive option are the scheduled cargo flights to the U.S. and cities of Central America from the international airport in Managua.

## Hurricane Mitch

On October 30, 1998 the progress Nicaragua had made towards improved economic growth was dealt a cruel blow. In a matter of days, heavy rains and winds that followed in the wake of Hurricane Mitch destroyed the country's harvests and the infrastructure which supported the agricultural sector. The Nicaraguan economy, in President Arnoldo Alemán's own words, was "on its knees".

A preliminary government report estimated the damage at more than $1.54 billion, a figure which included the rebuilding of roads, houses, schools and health centers. The loss of Nicaragua's main export crops rocked an already fragile economy. A bumper coffee harvest, an important hard currency earner, was washed away and at least a third of the bushes on plantations would not recover and would require replanting. Bananas, sugar and other cash crops were also

Hurricane Mitch survivors - they lost home and possessions in the floods     *Sean Sprague/PANOS Pictures*

wiped out. Nevertheless, the IMF and World Bank insisted on the importance of Nicaragua keeping to economic targets agreed before Mitch. And the country was told to continue with the implementation of structural reforms.

In the meantime a massive campaign focussed the world's attention on the "unnatural" disaster of Nicaragua's vast debt service repayments. A church-inspired initiative calling for the cancellation of the debts of the world's poorest countries created the momentum for a number of countries to announce a series of debt cancellation and relief packages. In December 1998 the Paris Club of creditor nations agreed to a moratorium of three years on Nicaragua's debt repayments.

### Nicaraguans in Exile

The clichéd vision of the U.S. as the land of opportunity has always attracted a steady flow of Nicaraguans. Like many people from the developing world, they went in search of a higher standard of living, but during the 1980s thousands left for political reasons. The vast majority headed for Miami, Houston or Los Angeles, where they largely worked in low-paid jobs in the service industry. In 1990, after the Sandinistas were driven from power, an estimated 120,000 Nicaraguans returned from the U.S. Many staggered through customs with huge American refrigerators, hi-fi systems, video cameras and even pedigree dogs in tow, the sort of fancy goods which most Nicaraguans had never seen before. Like many political migrants, they wanted to use their experience abroad and set up businesses in their own country. But for a large number of returnees the dream of riches in Nicaragua became a nightmare. Many lost money in failed business ventures, others just could not settle back into what they now regarded as a backward country. At least 30,000 disenchanted Nicaraguans packed their bags and returned to the U.S., where they picked up where they left off, serving at petrol stations and fast-food outlets.

### Made in the USA

The influx of Nicaraguans more accustomed to pizzas, milkshakes and hamburgers than tortillas, beans and rice has had an extraordinary effect on the pattern of imports. Manufactured, processed and consumer goods are flooding the country. While the lifestyle of a small elite has resulted in a consumer boom, which has spurred the construction of malls, restaurants and leisure facilities, the import bill has rocketed to over $1 billion. Supermarket shelves are bulging with an impressive range of expensive American produce. Even ice cream has found a market. Shops selling electrical equipment and cellular phones are opening. Car sales are booming, with the number of vehicles on the roads doubling since 1990.

There has also been a considerable increase in private investment, reflecting growing commercial confidence in the country as the influence of trade unions wanes and wages fall. The efforts of the UNO and Liberal Alliance governments to shake off the image of Nicaragua as politically unstable have paid off. However, growing problems of corruption may well scare away potential investors, if they are not brought under control. While President Alemán has acknowledged the gravity of the issue, which extends to the highest spheres of government, he has not yet taken decisive action to clean out his administration. In the meantime, Transparency International, an organization which monitors institutional corruption, has placed Nicaragua high on its list of countries in which bribery and dishonesty are rife.

### Free Trade Zones

The road from the capital's airport into downtown Managua takes you past the imposing gates of the country's first free trade zone, a well-guarded compound which housed over twenty factories in 1997. They are largely Far East-owned, although there are also North American and European companies on site producing a variety of clothing, footwear and jewelry for export. Almost 50,000 workers, mostly women, are employed to assemble pre-cut garments, stitch shoes or make up necklaces. The

Zonas Franca commercial estate

*Tina Gue/PANOS Pictures*

conditions are usually cramped and the noise created by the roar of industrial machinery and near-by aircraft is often deafening.

The expansion of Nicaragua's export processing business has only taken off recently, although it has long dominated the economies of the other Central American countries. The UNO government introduced incentives and generous tax concessions in 1990, with the aim of enticing foreign companies to set up in Nicaragua. Initially investors held back, concerned about the country's volatile political situation, the strength of the unions and poor infrastructure. Yet within a few years their fears subsided, interest picked up and the revenues of the free trade zone surged dramatically. The absence of U.S. quotas on exports from Nicaragua has proved particularly attractive to investors, especially from the Far East, who are otherwise unable to penetrate the American market.

The Liberal Alliance has placed huge emphasis on the development of free trade zones as a means to generate employment and income. But the benefits derived from the presence of foreign companies are limited. Both the wages of the workers and payments to the Nicaraguan government in the form of rent or taxes are low. In a fiercely competitive environment, increases in pay or overheads might result in the companies moving on, which of course they frequently do in response to more lucrative openings elsewhere. Production in the free trade zone is a tightly contained business, which has no wider impact on the Nicaraguan economy. Raw materials are rarely bought locally, but are flown in from outside the country.

The plight of the free trade zones' employees has frequently attracted the attention of journalists from around the world, as well as labor, human rights and women's organizations. Well-documented cases of exploitation, discrimination against union activists and sexual harassment in Nicaragua have forced the government and resident companies to make some efforts to comply with laws protecting people from arbitrary dismissal, long hours and dangerous working conditions. In February 1998 a Code of Ethics drawn up by the María Elena Cuadra Womens' Movement (MECWM), a group representing women in the free trade zones, was passed by ministerial resolution, which carries the force of law. The Code not only restates the government's commitment to the rights of workers, but grants MECWM a key role in an Independent Monitoring Group set up to ensure compliance with the country's laws. Illegal practices are now more likely to be reported by workers, who are becoming more confident of their rights as a result of the support of MECWM and their membership of trade unions, which are now operating more openly in many of the factories.

### Human Exports

Remittances sent back to their families by more than a million Nicaraguans working abroad make a huge contribution to the economy. Checks worth over an estimated $600 million a year regularly arrive from the U.S. and Central America. The largest single concentration of Nicaraguans is to be found in Costa Rica, where a relatively successful economy has depended on them as a source of cheap labor. A stable population of 300,000 expatriates swells to almost a half million during harvest times. A temporary workforce regularly journeys south to take jobs for very low wages and in harsh conditions on banana plantations and coffee farms. Until recently the immigration authorities have overlooked their unofficial presence for economic reasons, but as the market reaches saturation point, Nicaraguans are finding their entry into Costa Rica barred. In 1998 more than 50,000 people were turned back at the border.

In a more bizarre and desperate attempt to tackle the country's rising employment, the Alemán government has officially sanctioned the recruitment of 5,000 Nicaraguans for "export" to Taiwan. Despite the enormous costs of flying the workers half way around the world and the Asian economic crisis, the project has moved ahead. An advance party of 500 workers left for Taipei shortly after the agreement was announced in 1998. They were found jobs in the manufacturing and construction sectors, but it re-

La Recollección church, León

mains to be seen how the language barrier and cultural differences will be overcome. The scheme is just one aspect of growing Taiwanese involvement in Nicaragua, which alongside a generous aid package and investment program, is no doubt intended as a reward for its diplomatic recognition of Taipei rather than Beijing.

## Tourism

Visitors to Nicaragua's only 5-star beach resort at Montelimar on the Pacific coast could be forgiven for thinking they were in any tropical country. Miles from the nearest town, foreign tourists and well-to-do Nicaraguans retreat to the self-contained pre-fabricated complex, where for a flat rate they can consume unlimited amounts of food and drink. It is the new face of tourism that Nicaragua is hoping to cash in on in an attempt to boost its foreign exchange earnings. But tourism is not necessarily the cash cow of the Nicaraguan government's dreams. Although it is now one of the most important sources of foreign exchange, the revenues generated by tourism are tiny compared to those in other countries in Central America, which have well-developed tourist industries. Nicaragua faces stiff competition. To the south, Costa Rica offers an unrivalled array of eco-tourism choices and to the north Honduras and Guatemala boast marvellous Mayan ruins.

Nicaragua is nevertheless very beautiful. Vast stretches of unspoiled beaches on the Pacific coast are almost uninhabited, though difficult to reach. There are just a handful of coastal resorts catering to day-trippers or visitors to the few sea-front hotels. Inland, the historic cities of León and Granada boast impressive colonial squares and churches. On Lake Nicaragua boats drift through the Isletas of Granada and slightly more seaworthy craft head for the volcanic islands of Ometepe or Solentiname. In contrast to the dense jungle of the Atlantic coast, the Pacific is easily explored. But it is clearly the impenetrable rainforest on the eastern seaboard and the biological reserves of Bosawas and Si-A-Paz, home to a rich variety of wildlife, flora and fauna, which have the greatest potential to attract travelers.

The lack of a developed tourist industry in Nicaragua does make it, of course, an attractive destination for many individual travelers, and there has been a steady stream of these ever since the revolution. But it is the organized tours from Europe and North America that bring in the serious money and which the Nicaraguan authorities are attempting to lure away from their neighbors. The government has offered tax breaks to private investors, a move which has paid off with plans to build three major hotels in Managua. And the number of visitors to the country is increasing, up from 197,000 in 1993 to about 350,000 in 1997.

There are now a handful of operators based in Managua offering an increasing selection of tours, mainly focusing on eco-tourism, but many in the industry argue that Nicaragua will not really be a big player in international tourism until its infrastructure is developed. Montelimar is less than 40 miles from Managua, but the journey takes almost an hour and a half depending on the state of repair of the road. Even the Rio San Juan, which the Spanish and British sailed up to reach Lake Nicaragua from the Caribbean coast is now largely off the beaten track. A luxury hotel in El Castillo was forced to close down through lack of customers after the hydrofoil ferry service across Lake Nicaragua to the mouth of the river was stopped.

The tourism industry has benefited from the Nicaraguan returnees from the U.S. More people now speak English, and the expansion of American fast food outlets in Managua like Pizza Hut and McDonalds (which reopened in July 1998 following a self-enforced absence of twenty years) is adding a modicum of sophistication and know-how to the service industry. Most Nicaraguans are fiercely proud of their country and a warm welcome awaits tourists. There is, however, a lot of work to be done before the country becomes a premier tourist destination, and it looks it will be many years before significant numbers of people are willing to choose Nicaragua instead of its better-known neighbors.

### Nicaragua's Pipe Dream

For centuries, entrepreneurs have dreamed of bringing Nicaragua to the forefront of world trade by linking the country's Pacific and Atlantic coasts by canal. And although its rivers and lakes have always seemed naturally suited to the project, the canal has never been built. After the completion of the Panama Canal in 1914, the project lost much of its appeal. Even so, the idea has survived. As recently as 1996, a U.S.-backed consortium moved into small offices in Managua to oversee a feasibility study. Instead of plans for a waterway, which rival American and British interests had envisaged building in the nineteenth century, the consortium proposed a railway, using the latest container technology to transport freight between eastern and western seaboards. It was election year and politicians talked of nothing else. They looked to the "dry canal", an international trade route enveloped in a huge free trade zone, as a solution to the country's economic and unemployment problems. The project was enthusiastically supported, with few parties at all interested in even considering possible drawbacks, which included the destruction of large areas of tropical rainforest. However, when the feasibility study was finished, the offices closed and the plans were unceremoniously set aside. The dream of the trans-oceanic link will no doubt continue to capture people's imaginations, but their visions of the country as a flourishing trade center are likely to remain in the realm of fantasy, with or without the canal.

# 4    ENVIRONMENT: THE POWER OF NATURE

## Hurricane Mitch

When the rains and winds of Hurricane Mitch hit Nicaragua in October 1998, they cut into its fragile earth with ease. Sun-baked, largely treeless plains turned into swirling seas of mud, and vast volumes of water cascaded down denuded hillsides and volcanoes filled to bursting-point. La Casita, a volcano in the province of Chinandega exploded from the weight of rainwater, and landslides buried alive several hundred inhabitants in the surrounding villages.

Hurricane Mitch was an unstoppable force, but the destruction caused in its wake was not only of nature's making. It was also a product of decades of environmental abuse. Vast areas of Nicaragua's forests have been cut back by loggers, peasant farmers and ranchers, the land stripped bare of almost all vegetation, leaving it largely incapable of absorbing even moderate seasonal rains. It was therefore perhaps not surprising that a deluge of rain, equivalent to what would fall in a whole year, left the country under water for weeks.

The most urgent task post-Mitch was to ensure that farmers had the seeds and tools to plant their land in mid-1999, but the long-term challenge was always to rebuild the country on environmentally sound principles. Reclaiming the fertility of its land and managing its forests and natural resources would not protect Nicaragua from hurricanes, tidal waves or volcanic eruptions, but it would help prevent a disaster on the scale of Mitch and guard against a complete collapse of the country's damaged ecology.

The emphasis was, however, on resuming the production of cash crops as quickly as possible and increasing the exploitation of natural resources. The IMF insisted that Nicaragua keep to economic targets set before the onslaught of Mitch, and although some creditor nations cancelled or rescheduled some of its debt, the pressures to pursue profits remained immense. The economic and political fall-out from the latest and most serious natural disaster in Nicaragua for centuries looked set to occupy the government's agenda for some time to come.

## Geography of Nicaragua

The lasting image of Nicaragua, at least for the next few years, will be the scenes of devastation in the wake of Mitch, but it is a country with a rich diversity of landscapes. South of the worst-affected areas lies La Concepción volcano. It towers above the small town of Alta Gracia and remains to its

Damage cause by Hurricane Joan, Bluefields, 1988          *Sean Sprague/PANOS Pictures*

inhabitants a constant reminder of the power of nature. Although now dormant, its last eruption in the 1960s swept away the farms that feasted on the rich soils at its feet. At over 5,200 feet, La Concepción dominates the island of Ometepe and the surrounding fresh waters of Lake Nicaragua. Tracks to the top wind through the shade of lush tropical vegetation, maize plots and small banana plantations before opening out onto the unprotected and charred volcanic slopes. The chatter of green parrots and the chortle of howler monkeys swinging in the trees fade as the steep ascent begins.

La Concepción is just one of Nicaragua's many volcanoes, which form an impressive chain running the length of the country through the Pacific lowlands. Their rumblings are frequent, and sporadic eruptions can be a fatal intervention in people's lives. Managua, the capital, spans a seismic fault line, and although the city was destroyed in 1972 by a massive earthquake which killed an estimated 20,000 people, it was never moved to safer terrain. The ruins of the old city center have remained untouched. The shells of hotels, casinos and shops, once the playground of Latin America's rich, were left to decay. Now clusters of low-rise buildings and shantytowns spread haphazardly into the suburbs and are home to almost a million inhabitants. León, the country's second city, also lives under the constant threat of volcanic activity. It is within sight of Cerro Negro, one of several active volcanoes in the region, and has recently experienced the fall-out of eruptions. In 1991 and 1995 the town choked under clouds of volcanic ash for months before the rains finally cleared the air.

The peaks of the volcanoes overlook the flatter expanses of agricultural land on the Pacific coast and the mountainous terrain of central Nicaragua. More than two-thirds of country's 4.4 million population is concentrated on the western side of the country. The Pan-American Highway, the country's main truck route, is a vital link for the transportation of agricultural produce grown in the area. It starts in the pine forests on the Honduran border and cuts down through maize, tobacco, vegetable and rice fields before reaching the capital on the southern shore of Lake Managua, the edge of which it hugs all the way to Costa Rica in the south. The route is busy, but often in bad repair. Large container trucks, battered buses and sometimes even cattle-pulled carts grind to a halt while the single-line traffic negotiates the frequent pot holes.

In the mountainous central zone of the country, coffee plantations dominate the slopes. Rain is plentiful and well-fed dairy cattle graze verdant pastures. To the east, the roads built to transport the coffee gradually peter out and the terraced hillsides give way to tropical rainforest. A wide variety of precious hardwood trees stretch across more than half Nicaragua's land mass to the Atlantic coast, which is physically and culturally separate from the rest of the country. A journey from west to east, from the Pacific to the Caribbean coast, emphasizes the lack of communication between the two regions and demonstrates the very real obstacles in uniting them.

Travel overland from Managua to the Caribbean port of Puerto Cabezas, the provincial capital of the North Atlantic Autonomous Region (RAAN), requires time and patience. Despite the recent investment of foreign aid to upgrade the connection, the roads turn to mud during the rainy season and the bridges are often washed away as the rivers burst their banks. Efforts to improve the region's infrastructure were set back further by the damage caused by Hurricane Mitch to new construction work. The area is sparsely populated. The Miskito, the largest Indian group, are concentrated around Puerto Cabezas and along the Rio Coco, which marks the border with Honduras. A small number of Mayangna Indian communities are only accessible by canoe, although they increasingly live within reach of the towns and villages in the north-east of the country. A more easily negotiated route is by road to Rama at the mouth of the Escondido river and by boat onward to the coastal town of Bluefields, the capital of the South Atlantic Autonomous Region (RAAS). The area is dominated by the English-speaking creoles, who have mostly settled on the Caribbean coast and on the idyllic palm-fringed Corn Islands.

Cattle in the dry season, Ometepe, Lake Nicaragua   *Robert Francis/South American Pictures*

### The Advancing Agricultural Frontier

Nicaragua is often described as the "land of volcanoes and lakes" – a description which seems apt enough – but it is also the land of deforestation and dried-up rivers, an environmental time bomb that was ignited by the arrival of Hurricane Mitch. And unless the causes are seriously addressed in the near future, there is nothing to prevent further disasters.

Nicaragua is the biggest of the five Central American countries, yet despite its size (about 50,000 square miles), it is heavily dependent on imports to feed its growing population. Since the turn of the century, agricultural production geared toward export rather than domestic consumption has forced subsistence and small farmers from the most fertile areas of the Pacific plains. With less and less land available, poor peasants have migrated into the rainforest. Using "slash and burn" agriculture, they have quickly exhausted the fertility of the tropical soils, which are ill-suited to traditional crop production. As a consequence of rapidly declining yields, they have cut deeper into the jungle, pushing the agricultural frontier forward at an alarming rate.

It is not just small farmers who are causing environmental damage. Vast areas in the eastern province of Chontales have been given over to large-scale ranchers, who have moved in to raise cattle for the lucrative

North American market. On the western coastal strip, thousands of acres previously devoted to cotton, stand empty. The effect of so much land clearance has been devastating. With fewer trees, less water is retained by the earth and the top soil quickly dries out. The erosion that follows leaves the land largely infertile and increasingly inhospitable. Water courses, streams and even rivers are fast disappearing, and as they evaporate, stretches of countryside are destined to become desert.

## *Organic Farming*

Many small farmers who did not go down the "slash and burn" route have taken a more positive approach to production by adopting organic farming techniques. Although some people readily admit that they chose the option not because of environmental concerns, but because they simply could not afford to pay for expensive fertilizers and pesticides, it nevertheless created an enthusiastic organic movement that is still thriving today. Avelina Navarro is an example of how farmers with little land or capital can become self-sufficient. She has a small holding in the province of Madriz, high in the deforested hills of northern Nicaragua. Instead of applying chemicals, which are invariably imported from the U.S., she now sprays her crops with water-based solutions made from local plants in order to keep pests away. Her plot is lined with pretty marigold flowers, which as well as adding a riot of color, are more important for keeping insects away.

Like many other local farmers, Avelina Navarro has just started a compost heap made from household waste and chicken droppings. It fertilizes an impressive array of produce in her kitchen garden, including cabbage, onions, garlic, herbs, melons and tomatoes. Around her small plot of land she has planted yucca trees, which help to prevent heavy rains dragging away the richer top soils. Some of the techniques used by Avelina have been reclaimed from her indigenous past, while others have been learned from a number of organizations promoting environmentally sustainable agriculture.

One of the most influential farming organizations in Nicaragua today is UNAG, a farmers' and ranchers' union. Since its foundation in 1981, it has encouraged small producers like Avelina Navarro to farm environmentally through a program called *Campesino a Campesino* or Farmer to Farmer. The basic idea is for participants to share and pass on knowledge to other members of their communities, which will help improve the long-term sustainability of food production and management of natural resources. In this way hundreds of thousands of people have learned about the experience and innovations of organic farming. With support from UNAG, some small farmers have even begun to export organic produce including coffee and sesame to Europe and North America.

There is a wide range of projects providing incentives for people to abandon unsustainable farming practices and to protect their local environment. One very large challenge is to safeguard forests, which although most threatened by commercial logging, are also being slowly stripped back by people collecting firewood for domestic consumption. Everybody living in the countryside and even a high percentage of urban dwellers traditionally use very inefficient open stoves to cook on. UNAG, among other organizations, is promoting an alternative design, which reduces the consumption of fuel by almost half. Alongside its initiatives to reforest denuded areas and riverbanks, the project is making a small but important contribution to raising people's awareness of the country's shrinking natural resources.

## El Niño

While some efforts are being made to reverse environmentally damaging practices, Nicaragua faces yet another serious ecological problem, this time not of its own making. Much has been written about El Niño, a phenomenon causing dramatic global fluctuations in weather conditions, but few people in Nicaragua were prepared for the havoc it has caused. The country's subsistence farming has consequently been at a near standstill for several years. Rains that once arrived in May and fell through to November can no longer be relied on, and some parts of the country stand dry for many of these months.

The resulting drought and loss of crops have left large numbers of peasant families without food or seeds, even before Hurricane Mitch obliterated their harvests in 1998. Although international aid agencies have dramatically stepped up their emergency programs in response to the ensuing crisis, the combination of El Niño and the day-to-day destruction of the country's natural resources is likely to prevent its recovery. With the government heavily dependent on food aid, malnutrition among adults and children has become widespread. The Ministry of Agriculture estimated in 1995 that at least 40 percent of rural children under five were malnourished. Moreover, the figures are likely to get considerably worse as people tackle the mounting difficulties of survival without their traditional reserves – chickens and pigs – which were swept away in the floods.

## Fair Trade

Del Campo, a successful marketing co-operative in western Nicaragua, was successfully exporting sesame to a number of European countries, Japan, Canada and the U.S. before Hurricane Mitch struck. Certified organic sesame oil was also being sold through the Community Trade program of the Body Shop, a British-based cosmetics company, which promotes fair and environmentally sustainable trade. The future of Del Campo's exports was put under threat as the co-operative worked to resume production for its established international markets.

The provinces of Chinandega and León, where the 3,200 members of Del Campo's co-operatives live, incurred the greatest damage and highest loss of life in the country. Some 2,500 people died in the region following the floods. When the waters receded, the sesame farmers found that they had lost almost the entirety of their crop, and 90 percent of the certified organic production was immediately written off. Nevertheless, they were quick to recognize the potential of the high levels of moisture in the soil, which were ideally suited to the cultivation of sesame. In some of the worst affected areas, including Poseltega, a village which suffered huge loss of life in mudslides, co-operative members secured the funds to plant more than 1,200 acres of sesame by mid-December 1998.

With the exception of the deluge brought by Hurricane Mitch, Nicaragua has otherwise experienced extremely low rainfall. Hydroelectric plants, which provide a fifth of the country's electricity, have been working way below capacity. To make matters worse, Mitch destroyed five plants, which resulted in a further fall in production. Fortunately, since 1979 Nicaragua has sought to develop the tremendous potential of its volcanoes to generate the country's energy needs. A large geo-thermal station is located near the Momotombo volcano, an impressive and perfectly symmetrical cone which dominates the horizon north of Lake Managua. Its huge turbines are driven by the dry hot steams and vapors, which are permanently pushing their way through the rock strata to the earth's surface. There are plans to open new geo-thermal stations and make better use of the alternative energy source. In the meantime, imported oil makes up over half of Nicaragua's energy supply.

## Logging

The issue of the worldwide logging of forests has always been an important subject for environmentalists and pressure groups, but the focus of attention has inevitably fallen on the destruction of the largest forests like the Amazon in South America or those of Irian Jaya in Indonesia. The problem of logging in Nicaragua rarely receives serious attention, but it is causing immense environmental and social fall-out, albeit on a smaller scale. The rate of deforestation in Nicaragua is now so intense that some experts say the country's forest is disappearing ten times faster than the Amazon. While a third of the country is still covered in forest, the area is estimated to be shrinking at the rate of 400 square miles a year. It has been calculated that if the destruction continues at the prevailing rate, there will be no tropical forest in Nicaragua by 2025.

Murals have accompanied the Sandinista revolution and have provided the opportunity for many international volunteers to take part in their creation. Many murals have now been painted over by unsympathetic authorities, including by Arnaldo Alemán while he was mayor of Managua. But mural workshops remain, especially in Estelí, where they continue to be painted by children and adults as political and social commentary.

Sandinista mural, León
*Robert Francis/South American Pictures*

Painting a mural, Esteli
*Gary Willis/South American Pictures*

Carnival costume, Granada

*Jon Spaull/PANOS Pictures*

Carnival mask-maker, Masaya

*Sean Sprague/PANOS Pictures*

View of the old cathedral
and Lake Managua

*Jon Spaull/PANOS Pictures*

Catholicism plays a large part in the life of Nicaraguans. Even though there has been religious freedom since 1939, when Nicaraguans say 'the church', they mean the Roman Catholic Church. The church runs the greater part of the education system, although it is often the only contact people will have with the institution until their wedding, or more likely, their funeral.

Almost all villages, towns and cities hold annual fiestas to honor the saint of their choice and tradition. The traditions of parading giants or using masks during carnival are of uncertain origin, but certainly came over with the Spanish, and have been changed and adapted by life in Nicaragua. The importance of the church was clear in 1983 when half a million Nicaraguans, over an eighth of the population, came to Managua to see Pope John Paul II.

The new cathedral, Managua

*Jon Spaull/PANOS Pictures*

Mural in Managua

*Sean Sprague/PANOS Pictures*

Piñatas are a central feature of any Nicaraguan fiesta. They provide an explosion of colour in the markets where they are sold, with the brightly-coloured figures swaying en masse waiting to be taken to the children who will beat the hidden sweets out of them.

A piñata holding sweets is attacked at a fiesta, Matagalpa

*Paul Smith/PANOS Pictures*

The history of logging in Nicaragua is all too familiar. Transnational companies were granted large concessions on the Atlantic coast and in northern Nicaragua under the Somoza dictatorship. They made quick work of removing forests of mahogany, cedar, rosewood and logwood for sale on the international timber market. Fortunately, the industry was brought to temporary halt in the 1980s, when the Sandinista government established a Ministry of the Environment, which introduced legislation to protect the country's natural resources. It was a policy that paid dividends, with the operations of large logging projects reduced to a bare minimum. But the Sandinista conservation efforts were dealt a heavy blow in 1988, when Hurricane Joan hit the Central American isthmus. The winds destroyed an estimated 10 percent of the rainforest and largely reversed the achievements of the government's environmental policies.

In the 1990s, although the Nicaraguan government has continued to pay lip-service to environmental protection, successive administrations have succumbed to the temptation to exploit the country's abundant natural resources. Laws protecting the rainforest and the rights of people living in protected biological areas have been broken on a number of occasions. In 1996 a 30-year logging concession to clear rainforest along the north Caribbean coast was granted to Solcarsa, a subsidiary of the huge South Korean corporation Kum Kyung, in a move which provoked the outrage of environmentalists across the world. For $20 million Solcarsa bought an area of 150,000 acres, including an ancient tropical hardwood forest rich in mahogany. In order to extract the timber, a 120-feet wide road was built, destroying forest, watersheds and habitats for wildlife in the nearby Bosawas national reserve.

The government agreement with Solcarsa forcibly displaced Mayangna Indians in the village of Awas Tigni from their traditional lands and violated their constitutional right to determine the use of local resources. With the help of the Indian Law Resource Center, based in Washington DC, the villagers initiated legal proceedings to cancel the concession. The Nicaraguan courts eventually ruled in their favor in early 1998 and appeared to bring the long-running dispute to an end. However, with the approval of the government, logging in the rainforest continued. It was business as usual at the Solcarsa plywood plant in Rosita, although the trees were now cut under the watchful eye of the army and police. In the end, Solcarsa withdrew from Nicaragua in April 1998, not on account of its illegal trade, but due to financial difficulties after the company's shares collapsed on the Korean Stock Exchange.

La Luz gold mine *Paul Smith/PANOS Pictures*

## Mining

It is not just the logging companies that have exploited Nicaragua's rich offering of natural resources: mining corporations have also moved in for a share of the spoils. It was not always so. In the sixteenth century, the Spanish colonial authorities were dismissive of Nicaragua's gold and silver deposits and made little effort to tap the country's resources. But discoveries of gold in the 1920s proved that they had underestimated its mining potential. British and North American companies successfully extracted precious metals from an area in the northeast between Bonanza, Siuna and Rosita throughout the 1940s and 1950s. Although production tailed off and mines closed during the Contra war, the industry appears to be taking off once again. The government has sold a large number of concessions, but only a small percentage of the profits are returned for reinvestment in the damaged mining areas. There are serious concerns about the impact on the local environment, in particular, the flow of mercury and cyanide residues used in the extraction process of the metals into the region's rivers and water supplies.

## Atlantic Environmental Corridor

When the Nicaraguan government created the Bosawas national park in October 1991 and the United Nations certified the area of 3,000 square miles as a Biosphere Reserve, the hopes of environmentalists were raised. Money for the establishment of a protected corridor, running southwards from Bosawas in the northern department of Jinotega to the Río San Juan on the border with Costa Rica, was potentially available from the World Bank's Global Environmental Facility (GEF). But access to the funds was conditional on preparatory measures, such as the government undertaking the distribution of land titles to Indian communities living in the corridor. At the end of 1998 the task had not been carried out, a possible indication of waning enthusiasm for a project which would prevent the sale of exploitation rights to foreign logging and mining companies. However, if Nicaragua eventually meets the GEF criteria, the Atlantic Biological Corridor, as the area will be known, will form the first link in a chain of protected parks stretching from Guatemala to Panama.

### Threatened Species

Parrots brandished on sticks, toucans in bags and trembling chained spider monkeys are increasingly part of the paraphernalia of Nicaragua's booming street trade. Despite the laws protecting the animals and birds of the country's jungle, business is brisk and many exotic creatures end up as pets in the homes of the middle class.

Nicaragua has an impressive array of wildlife. Extensive shallow water habitats in the northeast of the country attract a bewildering range of fresh and salt-water fish, as well as large numbers of green and hawksbill turtles, manatees, crocodiles and caymans. Lake Nicaragua is home to sierra fish and the world's only freshwater sharks, while dolphins and whales are sometimes visible off the Pacific and Atlantic coasts. And the tropical forests are the natural habitat for the many different species of colorful birds and snakes, jaguars and howler monkeys. But, as in other parts of the world, there is an increasing number of animals which are being put onto the endangered species list, as the loggers, miners and commercial hunters, in their own separate ways, undermine the country's ecosystem.

### Cleaning Up Lake Managua

One local ecosystem that has already been destroyed almost beyond repair is the vast expanse of Lake Managua on whose shores the capital sits. The view across the lake from Managua is breathtaking. A sheet of still, shimmering blue water stretches to the foothills of the rugged mountains in Chontales. But the image of beauty and tranquillity is deceptive. After a while spent looking at the lake, the absence of fishing boats, pleasure craft or people washing or children playing in the water, becomes conspicuous. There is a good reason for this. The lake has long been badly polluted and its dangers are well known to local residents. Untreated sewage, industrial and agro-chemical waste have been pumped into the lake for decades. Mercury and metal traces deposited by a factory, no longer in business, have slowly killed the fish, which often float poisoned to the surface. Only the poorest risk casting their nets or using the water to irrigate their crops.

The task of reviving the lake is daunting, but a huge and expensive project, sponsored by the Inter-American Development Bank (IDB), aims to modernize Managua's sanitation system and clean the shoreline. A trip to the neighborhood of Acahualinca on the edge of the lake is a graphic enough example of what needs to be done. In the middle of the densely populated shantytown a huge sewage pipe is ruptured and the waste of a city's inhabitants courses past houses and runs directly into the lake. In the first stage of the IDB project, almost 30 miles of sewer mains, pumping stations and treatment facilities will be built to ensure the sanitary disposal of solid waste. Thereafter, the low-lying areas surrounding the lake will also be drained and leveled to eliminate mosquito breeding grounds in conjunction with a community education program. Despite these efforts, it is thought it could take up to 30 years before the lake is clean enough to fish or bathe in.

# 5    SOCIETY: CULTURE OF RESISTANCE

### People of the Pacific Coast

A curious blend of melodic Spanish music and mournful pre-Columbian tones fills the air. A masked character steps out into a packed town square to thunderous applause. He is *El Güegüense*, a peddler of mixed Indian and Spanish blood, the protagonist of a popular play written during the colonial period. With a low sweeping bow, he begins his story of misfortune and suffering under Spanish rule. Quick-witted, mischievous and sharp-tongued, the crowd laughs at his cunning and cheers his impudence.

*El Güegüense* is one of the earliest and most important pieces of writing about the fusion of the cultures of the indigenous Indians and the colonial Spanish. Their descendants, known as *mestizos*, now make up more than three-quarters of the Nicaraguan population. The play probably dates back to the mid-sixteenth century, when the mestizo class first began to emerge. Although nothing is known about the author, it clearly expressed the frustrations of a mixed-race people, who were looked down on and mistreated by the Spanish colonizers, who held the "purity" of their own blood in great esteem.

The play is still regarded as an important expression of Nicaraguan identity. The central character's clever use of language, word play and double meaning have become known as 'Nica' traits. His rebelliousness, disrespect for authority and sense of justice are also considered features of what constitute the stereotype of a Nicaraguan. Less positively, the idea of a duplicitous streak in the national psyche is derived from the peddler's ability to dupe and outwit the authoritarian figure of the Governor Tastuanes. The ability to say one thing while thinking another has even been used to explain why the Sandinistas surged ahead in the opinion polls but lost the 1990 elections. Whether you take the psychology of the Güegüense seriously or not, he remains a widely celebrated symbol of the country's culture. Brightly clad wooden carvings of the play's characters line the stalls of the craft market in Masaya, and life size statues take pride of place on the roundabout of the Plaza España in Managua.

The inhabitants of the Pacific side of the country are almost exclusively mestizos. There are a small number of Indian communities in Subtiava, a neighborhood of León and in the central highlands of Matagalpa and Jinotega, but they have retained few characteristics of their pre-conquest culture and their native languages are long since dead. But even though Spanish rule brought a brutal end to indigenous customs, traditions and worship, the stories about the conquerors' cruelty have survived and incorporate many of the mythical figures and gods revered by the Indians before colonialism. The restless souls of conquistadors, headless priests and witch-like women are among a host of characters who recall the horror of the colonial period and haunt the Nicaraguan imagination.

### People of the Atlantic Coast

In contrast with the Pacific coast, the Atlantic coast is characterized by the diversity of its ethnic groups and cultures. However, none of its indigenous Indians, the creoles or the Garifuna have ever regarded themselves as Nicaraguan and they have resisted attempts by the administration in Managua to bring them under centralized control since the country's independence in 1821. The costeños, as the people on the Caribbean side of Nicaragua prefer to be known, have struggled to protect their own cultures and have more readily identified with Britain, the former colonial power, or the U.S. than with Nicaragua. Even today, English and Miskito, an indigenous Indian language, are more widely spoken than Spanish outside the growing mestizo population on the coast.

The thick jungle and forest on the eastern side of the country provided a natural defense against invading forces and the influence of outsiders. Although the British occupied the Atlantic coast for centuries, they made no attempt to assert direct control of the region and exploited its resources through an alliance with the Miskito, one of three indigenous Indian groups. Their intervention and support for the Miskito, who some say were named after the muskets they acquired from the British, resulted in the demise of the Rama and Mayangna Indians, who were hunted and sold as slaves. The settlers were less zealous than the Spanish about imposing their faith on their subjects, but contact with the British and missionaries, who followed in their wake, began to erode the regions' traditional way of life.

The Miskito lived communally before outsiders reached their communities. There was no concept of private property and the land and natural resources of the region were used by the community as a whole. A Council of Elders, made up of the more senior members of the group, advised on political and moral issues. Yet, as Miskitos were converted in increasing numbers by Moravian missionaries in the nineteenth century, the authority of their own forms of government waned and pastors became the key figures in their communities. Although they were encouraged to accept the notion of individual ownership, their collective relationship with the rainforest and their emphasis on living in harmony with nature have still not broken down and are enduring features of Miskito culture.

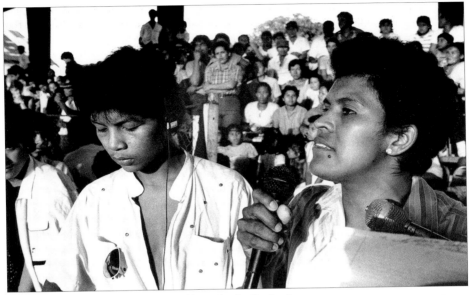

Miskito Indians protest against threat of loss of collective lands        *Julio Etchart/PANOS Pictures*

The Miskitos are still the largest indigenous group on the Atlantic coast, with an estimated population of between 80,000 and 100,000. They are concentrated in the northeast of the country along the Rio Coco, which marks the border between Nicaragua and Honduras and divides the Miskito community across national boundaries. Inland from Puerto Cabezas, there are approximately 8,000 Mayangna Indians, who are sometimes pejoratively known to outsiders as Sumo, the word for cowardly in their language. Some 1,400 Ramas, the smallest Indian group, live on Rama Cay, an island in Bluefields Bay, which they acquired as a reward for their services to the Miskito during the British colonial period. Although their numbers have expanded in the last decade, their language will probably be lost in the near future as it is now only spoken by no more than twenty elderly Ramas.

### Black Nicaraguans

The creoles are the descendants of white settlers and black slaves brought to the Atlantic coast by the British in the eighteenth century. They were kept below the Miskito in the ethnic hierarchy of the Atlantic coast until Britain withdrew from the region in the mid-nineteenth century. Thereafter, the creoles improved their economic position and superseded the Miskito as the dominant political class. Even today, Nicaragua's 30,000 creoles, comprising approximately twenty percent of the Atlantic coast's population, are still far more prosperous and better educated than any of the other ethnic groups. The Garifuna, descendants of black slaves and Indians in the region, number no more than 3,000 in Nicaragua. They live alongside the creole community in Pearl Lagoon and use creole English rather than the Garifuna language spoken by communities in Belize and Honduras.

The creole community identifies closely with the English-speaking Caribbean and is concentrated along the coast around Puerto Cabezas, Bluefields, the Corn Islands and Pearl Lagoon. The atmosphere is very different from the Pacific's. Here people live at a more relaxed pace and dance to reggae music rather than salsa. An annual celebration in May attracts people from far and wide. Basing the event on the English tradition of maypole dancing, the creoles have transformed it almost beyond recognition, and energetic participants twist around colorfully decorated maypoles to the accompaniment of loud African rhythms.

### Separate and Different

The Atlantic coast was formally incorporated into Nicaragua when the country became independent, but the central government always tended to neglect the region, interested only in exploiting its natural resources. Even under the Somoza dictatorship, the region was largely left to its own devices and its inhabitants were mostly unaware of the repressive forces at work on the Pacific. Very few *costeños* were involved in the 1979 revolution and the declared interest of the FSLN's leaders in integrating the Atlantic coast with the rest of the country was met with skepticism. Although improvements in the region's infrastructure, health services and opportunities for education were welcomed, the Sandinista government was often insensitive to ethnic concerns and lacked understanding of the indigenous culture. The authorities made a number of mistakes, the most serious of which was the forced and unwelcome relocation of 10,000 Miskito Indians in 1982. In a move that generated enormous hostility, they were transferred for their safety away from the war zone along the border to Tasba Pri, a government-built settlement.

The Sandinista government's heavy-handed dealings on the coast and the economic hardships brought about by the U.S. blockade fuelled long-harbored aspirations for independence among the people of the Atlantic coast. The imposition of military service was especially unpopular and thousands of Miskito took up arms to fight for autonomy. Some even joined the counter-revolution and fought alongside the Contras. Although human rights organizations reported violations against the Miskito, Washington's grossly exaggerated claims of ethnocide backfired when the

Miskito girl grinding corn, San Jeronimo

*Sean Sprague/ PANOS Pictures*

U.S. State Department produced photographs of tortured bodies, which were later shown to be those of Sandinistas killed by the Somoza dictatorship. Nevertheless, the FSLN government reassessed the situation and adopted a more enlightened policy, which eventually laid the foundations for a degree of political autonomy on the Atlantic coast.

### Autonomy

Provisions for self-rule were included in Nicaragua's new Constitution, which became law in 1987. In response, most Miskito disarmed and prepared to participate in the election of two regional assemblies based in Puerto Cabezas and Bluefields. But those Miskito allied with the Contras did not return to civilian life until the end of the Contra war in 1990, when voting was finally able to take place. An indigenous party, YATAMA, was formed and was initially successful at the polls. Even so, the transfer of power has been fraught with problems and the frustrations of sharing the responsibilities of government with the Pacific authorities have created conflict. Infighting and differences in opinion have since split the ethnic vote and allowed the FSLN, and more recently the Liberal Alliance, to win power.

The relationship between the central government and the Atlantic coast broke down completely in 1997, when the Liberal Alliance suspended funding to the regional assemblies, which have been unable to meet on a regular basis ever since. In the meantime a Council of Elders has set up a parallel governing body based in Puerto Cabezas, which they have named by its indigenous name, Bilwi. The government's blatant abuse of the autonomy laws and the encroachment of foreign logging and mining companies into the ancestral lands of the indigenous Indians have provoked a hardening of attitudes. An increasing number of *costeños*, particularly Miskito, now support breaking away from Nicaraguan rule completely and declaring the Atlantic coast independent.

## *Religion*

The crumbling grandeur of Nicaragua's churches is a reflection of the power the Catholic Church wielded in its heyday. León boasts the largest cathedral in Central America. But if the story passed down the generations is to be believed, the imposing building was intended for Lima, in Peru, the center of the Spanish Empire at the time. The plans were somehow erroneously dispatched to Nicaragua and the monumental task of construction painstakingly started in the 1740s and carried on for over an entire century. Whether the tale is true or not, the Spanish colonial authorities used religion as a means of control in Nicaragua with great effect. And the Church dutifully colluded in preaching subservience to its Indian congregations, who were obliged to convert and attend services. Church leaders were extremely rich and supportive of the conservative ruling classes – a relationship which endures to this day despite the fact that Nicaragua became a secular state in 1939.

The hierarchy of the Catholic Church in Nicaragua has rarely spoken out against the status quo. It remained passive even in the face of the Somoza dictatorship and its bishops only added their voices to the growing opposition movement in the late 1970s. In contrast, the lower orders of the Church, influenced by the radical doctrines of liberation theology, actively supported the Sandinista revolution. Many priests and nuns played a particularly vital role in the urban insurrection, acting as messengers and providing shelter for the FSLN guerrillas. After the triumph of the 1979 revolution, a number of clergy were given important positions in the FSLN government. Miguel D'Escoto, a Maryknoll priest, held the post of Foreign Minister throughout the 1980s; Ernesto Cardenal, a monk on the Solentiname islands of Lake Nicaragua, became the Minister of Culture; and his brother, Fernando Cardenal, a Jesuit helped organize the Literacy Crusade before taking over as the Minister of Education.

While the priests in the FSLN government maintained that there were no contradictions between Christianity and the revolution, the Vatican was of a very different opinion. When Pope John Paul II touched down on Nicaraguan soil in March 1983, he condemned the political involvement of Father D'Escoto and the Cardenal brothers, criticized the popular church and refused to bless people killed by the Contras. His hostility to the FSLN severely disappointed a crowd of over half a million and confirmed the growing and irreconcilable rift between the Sandinistas and the Catholic hierarchy. Not long afterwards the revolutionary government closed a right-wing Catholic radio station and expelled ten foreign priests and the Nicaraguan Bishop Vega from the country for openly supporting the counter-revolution.

The defeat of the Sandinistas in 1990 ended the dispute with Rome and signaled the return of the hierarchy's influence within the highest levels of government. The fresh start was marked by the construction of the new and extremely modern cathedral in Managua with money raised in the U.S. The Church, headed up by Cardinal Obando y Bravo, an arch-conservative renowned for his support for the Contras, played a part in the election of both the Chamorro and Alemán governments. In the 1996 elections, just days before people voted, Obando y Bravo made a point of celebrating a televised mass with Alemán, the Liberal Alliance's candidate. In return for his support, the government has since allowed the Cardinal's extremely conservative ideology to shape some of its policies and bring its institutions more firmly in line with official Catholic teachings.

Although most Nicaraguans regard themselves as Catholics, the vast majority of people rarely attend church on a regular basis. Patron Saint celebrations attract large crowds, but for most people the colorful processions and street festivities are more about having a good time than exercising any religious belief. Only a small proportion of Nicaraguan Catholics ever receive the sacraments and their participation in spiritual activities is usually limited to baptisms and funeral rites. The relatively low ratio of Catholic priests to the professed number of believers reflects their declining influence and they remain more thinly spread than in almost any other Latin American country.

### Protestant Churches

For centuries the Catholic Church dominated the spiritual life of Nicaragua on the Pacific coast, aggressively driving Protestant missionaries away. Ministers of other denominations were sometimes even attacked. But by the early twentieth century, the Assembly of God, the Baptists and Episcopalians among others succeeded in establishing themselves. Their churches experienced a massive expansion in the 1950s and 1960s. It was the more fundamental and morally conservative evangelical groups from North America, encouraged by Somoza as a bulwark against the spread of Communism, that grew the fastest. In the 1980s, after the departure of most foreign missionaries hostile to the Sandinista revolution, the Protestant churches were run by Nicaraguans and continued to increase in size. Nowadays, a third of the population belongs to one or another of the country's numerous Protestant denominations. The boom in membership is even reflected in some towns, where old cinemas have been reopened as new theaters of evangelism.

On the Atlantic coast, on the other hand, the Protestant churches have held sway since the arrival of Moravian missionaries in 1847. The New Testament and other worship materials were translated into the language of the Miskito, among whom the Moravian Church attracted a strong following. It also provided for people's physical, as well as spiritual health, and opened clinics and schools, which in the absence of government provision were highly valued. In general, a more liberal mood prevails on the Atlantic coast and the Moravians have worked successfully alongside the Episcopalian Church, which is more popular with the creole population. The leaders of both churches maintained reasonably good relations with the FSLN government, openly speaking out against U.S. support for the Contras, and have supported *costeño* aspirations to greater regional autonomy.

### Arts and Literature

The poverty of Nicaragua often pulls a veil over the creativity of Nicaraguans and their love of the arts. The country has a rich artistic tradition, which thrives despite economic difficulties. Since the birth of Rubén Darío in 1867, Nicaragua has acquired a reputation as a land of poets. Darío, one of Latin America's most famous writers, was the first of the continent's modernist poets to experiment with free verse, symbolism and sensual imagery. Nicaragua's only air-conditioned theater, on the shore of Lake Managua, is named after him.

In the twentieth century Nicaragua has produced several internationally acclaimed poets and writers. Sergio Ramirez, vice-president in the Sandinista government, has written over 25 books, many of which have been translated into English and other languages. They are often found on the shelves of bookshops in the U.S. and Britain alongside the novels of Gabriel García Márquez and Carlos Fuentes. In common with many Latin American authors, Ramirez's works are largely inspired by political events, and Nicaragua's liberation struggle and the revolution are prominent themes in his writing. After the defeat of the FSLN in 1990, Ramirez formed his own political party before retiring from politics and devoting himself to his career as an author. His latest novel, *Margarita, está linda la mar* (Margarita, the sea is lovely), published in 1998, deals with the life of Ruben Darío and the assassination of Anastasio Somoza. Margarita was the name of Somoza's wife.

Another important figure on Nicaragua's literary scene is Father Ernesto Cardenal, who although told as a Trappist monk that he could not write, is widely recognized as one of Latin America's great poets. Following his ordination as a priest, Father Cardenal helped set up a monastic commu-

Statue of Rubén Darío

*Tony Morrison/South American Pictures*

nity in 1966 on the remote islands of Solentiname, where he spent his life working alongside the poor and encouraging artistic expression through painting and poetry. A school of primitive art was started and became famous for its colorful canvases and crafts. Increasingly politicized, Father Cardenal joined the FSLN and after the involvement of several community members in a Sandinista guerrilla attack on San Carlos in 1977, Solentiname was destroyed by the National Guard. The death of some of the young men, who fell in battle, inspired poems by Father Cardenal and other Nicaraguan poets. The Solentiname community was rebuilt in the 1980s and is still going today.

After the triumph of the Sandinista revolution, Father Cardenal accepted the post of Minister of Culture. Always dressed in jeans, a white cotton shirt and a beret, during the 1980s he put his creative talents into orchestrating a government-sponsored revival of the arts. Poetry, painting, music and dance courses were run from cultural centers and volunteers traveled the country taking their art forms to remote rural communities. Newly literate people published their works in a magazine produced by the Ministry of Culture and were given access to the literature and poetry of other Latin Americans through mobile libraries. As the costs of the Contra war escalated, however, funding for the arts was cut. Even the prestigious Rubén Darío theatre in Managua was closed.

Although the Sandinistas breathed fresh life into Nicaragua's arts, little evidence of cultural activity remains at the grassroots level today. Financial support from the government for aspiring painters, writers or actors dried up, and foreign donors are hard-pressed in the current climate to justify putting even small amounts of money into maintaining the country's cultural traditions. Ernesto Cardenal, however, even though he stepped back from politics in 1990 and returned to a more contemplative life of prayer, painting and writing, has remained an active advocate of support for the arts.

Since the 1979 revolution a growing number of women writers have come to prominence. Gioconda Belli is one of the best known. She has published several books of poetry and three novels, the latest in 1996, *Waslala: Memorial del Futuro*. Belli is a strong feminist, who occasionally writes for the Nicaraguan press, although she now lives in the United States. In keeping with her bold style of journalism, Belli published a three-part interview in 1998 with Zoilamérica Narváez in El Nuevo Diario about her accusations of sexual abuse against Daniel Ortega, her step father.

## Music

Wherever you go in Nicaragua, there is likely to be music. The country moves to the beat of salsa and the sounds of well-worn recordings blast from makeshift homes, market stalls and rickety buses. On Saturday evenings bars and dance halls fill with people eager to dance. Men invariably down large quantities of *Flor de Caña*, an excellent Nicaraguan rum, or home-made and potent brews made from maize. Seemingly lifeless bodies slumped across doorways or collapsed in ditches are a common sight.

Gatherings around guitars still take place in people's homes, although many people have been forced to sell their musical instruments to make ends meet or to pay family debts. And reflecting the times, the songs of the revolutionary struggle with their politically optimistic lyrics are no longer appropriate and seldom heard. But in their day, they were a powerful weapon of the Sandinista revolution. When the FSLN began to inflict serious damage on the Somoza dictatorship in the 1970s, the brothers Carlos and Luis Enrique Mejía Godoy from Madriz were busy putting instructions for assembling rifles and the call for insurrection into song. They no doubt ensured that a large number of illiterate and novice soldiers were better prepared for battle.

## The Garand

**Among all the rifles this garand is the best.**
**Its barrel caliber is 30,06**
**If you want to break it down, follow these instructions**
**to the letter,**
**Keep your eyes open for informers and listen to this song**
**Its powerful projectile travels as far as five blocks;**
**it weighs ten pounds exactly; eight bullets fit a clip.**
**The garand is made up of three pieces and they are**
**firing mechanism, gas cylinder and the barrel**
**First we must place the pieces of the rifle lined up neatly**
**from left to right.**
**It's better this way.**

First we take out the clip and we check it out well,
because sometimes a bullet in the chamber can cause an accident.

We pull the trigger guard by the trigger down a little and back.
The firing mechanism comes sliding out.
In a second we take off the stock from the barrel.
We take the trigger guard and unscrew the gas plug.
Now we disconnect the whole stopper.
Let's go on to the next step.
I take out the gas cylinder from its fitting;
next we take off the lower hand grip, and pulling the metal rod,
I take it off from the bottom of the barrel.

The bolt and slide can be taken apart and this blessed slide
comes right out of its position
and this way, *compitas*, the operation is finished.
Now we love our rifle so we can finish off the oppressor.

Carlos Mejía Godoy, From *Guitarra Armada*, Rounder Records, U.S.

Other less militaristic songs won the Godoy brothers broader appeal at home and abroad. They both worked for the Ministry of Culture during the 1980s, running music workshops and were part of a movement that sought to reclaim the country's folklore and traditions. Instruments such as the marimba, a huge wooden xylophone, gave their music a more indigenous feel. *Nicaragua Nicaraguita*, written by Carlos Mejía Godoy, became the country's unofficial anthem during the Sandinista years in power and was recorded by the British singer Billy Bragg following his visit to Nicaragua on a cultural delegation. In progressive Christian circles the *Misa Campesina*, a Nicaraguan peasant mass, also composed by Carlos Mejía Godoy, was extremely popular and is still widely performed. Nowadays, the brothers continue to perform and can be heard live in Managua's few clubs and annually in a benefit concert for Los Pipitos, an organization working with cerebral palsy children.

## Sport

There is really only one sport that arouses people's passions in Nicaragua: baseball. A trip to the national stadium in Managua takes you to the country's best-maintained and most carefully protected grass lawn, the hallowed baseball diamond. While the majority of other countries in Central America have football as the main sport, Nicaragua (like Panama) has opted for baseball. It was probably brought to Nicaragua by the American

Playing baseball in a rural community, Nueva Guinea

*Julio Etchart/PANOS Pictures*

marines, who occupied the country for most of the first half of the twentieth century.

Nicaragua still has a long way to go before it matches the great baseball nations such as the U.S. or Cuba, but it has recorded some notable recent successes. In the Olympic Games in Atlanta in 1996, the national team, known as *La Selección*, won a number of important matches and just missed out on a bronze medal after being beaten by the U.S. In 1998, the team came third in the World Championships held in Italy, behind Cuba and South Korea (yet another country to pick up the baseball bug from the U.S.). The country's greatest baseball achievement, however, is Dennis Martínez, who in August 1998 became the most successful Latin American pitcher in the history of U.S. major league baseball. His fans in Nicaragua call him *El Presidente*, following rumors that he was set to return to his native country in 1996 and enter politics.

While the cream of Nicaragua's baseball stars can often be seen practicing on the National Stadium's diamond, practitioners of the country's second most popular sport are hard at work in far from ideal conditions in the cavernous gaps beneath the stadium's grandstands. It is here that pugilists at Nicaragua's premier boxing club hone their art. The facilities are basic: paint cans filled with cement and joined by a metal bar act as barbells, plastic bags make sad-looking sweatsuits, and the pairs of gloves that are handed from one boxer to the next are often threadbare.

It is perhaps not surprising that in a country as poor as Nicaragua, boxing has such a strong following. It is one of those sporting clichés that the lucky few can box their way out of the ghetto to undreamed-of riches. And that is exactly what two of Nicaragua's most successful boxers have accomplished. Alexis Argüello, one of nine children, learned to fight on the streets of Managua. He went on to win three world titles in different weights during the 1970s and was undefeated in sixteen defenses. Rosendo Alvarez, like Argüello, became a world champion in the 1990s and defended his title successfully on several occasions. Unlike Argüello, he stayed in Nicaragua during the Sandinista years, when boxing was banned, and was enlisted into the army.

A footnote in Nicaraguan sport belongs to football. In a country where little is spent on sport, football gets a minor cut of the financial pie and little or no effort has been put into its development. As though to emphasize the extent to which the sport is cut off from the mainstream, you have to travel for 40 minutes outside Managua to the national football stadium in the southern town of Diriamba. It was at the Cacique Diriangén stadium that Nicaragua's attempt to proceed on the long road to qualifying for the World Cup Finals in France in 1998 faltered. A one-nothing defeat against Guatemala in May 1996 was followed by a two-one defeat in the return leg in Guatemala City a week later, putting Nicaragua's World Cup dreams on hold for another four years. In reality, it is unlikely that the national team will ever make it to the finals and emulate its football-crazy neighbors Honduras and Costa Rica.

### Media and the Internet

In towns and cities across Nicaragua you can hear the daily newspaper arriving from a distance. Carrying newspapers stacked high on their heads, hawkers call the name of the papers as they zigzag their way up and down neighborhood streets. On offer are a number of national titles: *La Prensa*, *Barricada*, *El Nuevo Diario* and *La Tribuna*. They each maintain tightly defined political allegiances – *Barricada* is owned by the FSLN and *La Prensa* has backed UNO and then the Liberal Alliance over the last decade. With political messages to be promoted, it is rare that the top stories coincide in all four main papers. If *La Prensa* is reporting on President Alemán meeting a foreign leader, *Barricada* might lead with Daniel Ortega's latest parliamentary performance.

Newspapers are expensive and none has a large circulation. Most people listen to the radio or turn on the growing number of television sets which have appeared in even the poorest of houses. Like the print media, radio and television stations are often extremely partisan. During the 1996 elections, when one of the right-wing channels was broadcasting President Alemán's victory speech, the Sandinista-owned channel was re-running a documentary about the 1979 revolution. Politics are rife on the airwaves, but this does not stop Nicaraguans getting their fill of soap operas or *telenovelas*, which are imported from Latin America. The Brazilian ones are usually the most popular, but a recent favorite from Colombia about a group of *cumbia-* and salsa-singing sisters has taken the country by storm.

While the political parties have successfully controlled large parts of the print and broadcast media, the same can not be said for the Internet, which by its nature spurns state interference. The Internet is slowly becoming more widespread in Nicaragua, spurred on by an increasing number of non-governmental organizations going on-line and by a surprisingly good telecommunications network, probably the best in Central America. The range of organizations, businesses and individuals maintaining sites is growing all the time, but as in other developing, and indeed developed, countries, sites tend to appear and disappear in an unpredictable fashion.

# WHERE TO GO, WHAT TO SEE

Nicaragua is a beautiful, although largely unexplored country. Even before its emerging infrastructure was laid to waste by Hurricane Mitch, it was frequently passed over by tourists as undeveloped and difficult to travel in. Although the destruction caused by a week of the heaviest rains in the country's history added to the challenges of discovering Nicaragua, it remains a fascinating place, steeped in history and driven by a passion for politics.

While the reconstruction effort will take years if not decades, it will be the poorest Nicaraguans living in the rural areas who bear the brunt of the disaster, not the more privileged classes or indeed visitors to the country. Only a month after Hurricane Mitch struck, a BBC correspondent filed a report remarking on the normality of life and questioning whether the media had overstated the crisis. While the Pan-American Highway and major roads essential to the country's economy were reopened within weeks, the rebuilding of minor roads, bridges and the tens of thousands of homes washed away in rural areas will depend on the generosity of the donor community.

In the meantime, most tourist destinations can be reached and services are back to normal. Managua, the capital, continues to provide the best facilities for richer tourists as well as the more modest needs of back-packers. But despite the trappings of fast-food restaurants, cinemas and air-conditioned rooms, it is probably not a place to stay in for weeks unless you have something specific to do. The main attractions of the capital are the fading grandeur of Revolutionary Square, the crumbling old cathedral and the beautifully restored National Assembly building, now the Palace of Culture, which houses an art collection, some sculpture and the occasional exhibition. In nearby fields the scattered ruins from the 1972 earthquake lie in the long grass. The Rubén Dario theatre and the Malecón, a lakeside promenade are a pleasant stroll away.

Away from the tranquility of Managua's old center, the bustle of the capital's markets provide an insight into the lives of ordinary people. But before diving in to soak up the atmosphere, be sure to leave your valuables behind. The Mercado Oriental market is notorious for muggings and is best left off your itinerary. The Roberto Huembes market is the safest and friendliest, with a large crafts section selling naive art, leather and pottery typical of Nicaragua. Most of the artifacts are made in Masaya, a pretty town just outside Managua and if you have the time, it's well worth the journey – stop on the way to visit Volcano Masaya, one of Nicaragua's live volcanoes.

Concepción volcano, Ometepe island, Lake Nicaragua          *Robert Francis/*
                                                            *South American Pictures*

Buses out of the capital leave from a number of markets. There are direct routes to the country's main towns with the exception of Bluefields and Puerto Cabezas on the Atlantic Coast, which are best reached by air. Overland travel is difficult, but far more adventurous. The journey to Bluefields starts in Rama and takes you down the River Escondido through the rainforest. But despite the maze of waterways, the trip to Puerto Cabezas relies on unpaved roads, which are almost impossible to negotiate in the rainy season.

Visits into the protected jungle areas of Bosawas in the northeast or Si A Paz on Nicaragua's border with Costa Rica require careful organization and guides. With the discovery in October 1998 of 62 basalt pillars in the southeast of the country, the site might well become part of the tourist circuit in the future. The impressive 36-foot-high columns, initially thought to be the ruins of an ancient Chiba city, are in fact the work of nature.

On the Pacific side of Nicaragua travel is straightforward. León, with its splendid colonial architecture, historically home to the Liberal Party, is an hour away from Managua. The largest cathedral in Central America faces out onto the central square, which was recently refurbished. There you can sit under the shade of orange trees and watch life go by. The surrounding streets and churches are fun to wander through, and the university, a hotbed of resistance during the Somoza dictatorship, is worth stepping into for the brightly colored murals painted during the 1980s.

León is blistering hot whatever the time of year, but the breezes of the Pacific Ocean are just a twenty-minute ride away. Poneloya is a small palm-lined resort with white sand beaches. However, powerful undercurrents make swimming extremely dangerous and most people sit at a respectful distance and watch, sometimes from the shade of a handful of weathered restaurants serving fresh fish and beer. There are other larger and more developed coastal resorts further south, but the low-rise complex of thatched beach cabins and swimming pools at Montelimar is about as built-up as it gets. Masachapa, Pochomil and San Juan del Sur are fishing villages with basic accommodation and eateries to cater for a modest flow of visitors. But during Holy Week don't expect to have more than leg-room on the beach, as Nicaraguans traditionally escape the closing stages of the dry season and arrive in droves to enjoy the sea air.

Granada, situated on the edge of Lake Nicaragua and looking out over an archipelago of hundreds of small islands, attracts a large number of day-trippers from Managua and tourists straying over the boarder from Costa Rica. It is also the starting point for stays on the volcanic islands of Ometepe, where some interesting eco-tourist initiatives are developing the potential of its tropical setting. Boats depart daily for the sleepy towns of Alta Gracia and Moyogalpa and less frequently for the islands of Solentiname further south. They invariably make the return journey heavily laden with plantains for sale on the mainland.

In the mountainous north of Nicaragua, pleasant temperatures make hiking an inviting activity, although it is not something that local people ever do for relaxation. Selva Negra, an alpine-style lodge set in the forest near Matagalpa is a perfect base for walking and serves excellent food. Further north, the provincial capitals of Estelí and Ocotal are also good places in which to stretch your legs, explore and climb the surrounding hills.

Traveling independently in Nicaragua requires taking the initiative, occasionally roughing it and making your own entertainment. Contact with Nicaraguans is easy and it helps to have some Spanish, as English is only spoken on the Atlantic coast. There are a growing number of language schools in Managua and in most of the main towns, which offer accommodation with Nicaraguan families and meetings with development, women's and human rights organizations as well as lessons. There are also study tours and work brigades organized by groups in the U.S. and Britain, and, of course, some commercially organized tours.

# TIPS FOR TRAVELERS

### Customs

Nicaraguans are tactile and expressive people. They greet each other with kisses, although men usually restrict themselves to handshakes and hugs with each other. But when it comes to other courtesies such as queuing for buses, it's a matter of push and shove. Don't be surprised to find yourself without a seat or even left behind unless you're prepared to stand your ground. Although time-keeping is often lax, you'll find buses usually leave on time and that people are reasonably punctual in work situations.

### Safety

It used to be safe to walk the streets of Managua at any time of day or night. Sadly, that is no longer true. Muggings are common and tourists need to take care wherever they are. Wandering into unknown residential areas, particularly in the poorer parts, is not recommended. Finding your way around Managua is difficult, and it is probably best to use taxis rather than buses for reasons of safety and efficiency. Outside of the capital, life is more easy-going and strolling in the streets, even at night, is usually an enjoyable experience.

### Taxis

Before taking a taxi, agree with the driver to a price for your destination. If it's off the beaten track, be sure you have good instructions as to how to get there. Giving directions is often difficult and requires an intimate knowledge of the capital. Managuans do not use street names. Instead they use torturously long addresses such as "from where the post office used to be, two blocks east and three blocks towards the lake, 50 yards west".

### Health

If you want to play safe it's best to stick to bottled water or carbonated drinks, which are widely available. Food from roadside or market stalls is probably best avoided. Nicaragua is not a high-risk malaria area, but precautions are still advisable, especially in the rural areas.

### Eating

Nicaraguans are not great gourmets, but many vegetables and fruits, such as yucca, green plantains, *pitahaya* and *jocote*, a type of plum, will seem exotic to the North American and European traveler. *Nacatamales* are a specialty made with a maize dough, but there are scores of tasty corn-based dishes worth searching out. The staple food is *gallo pinto*, a mixture of rice and beans and tortillas made from maize flour. Western-style cuisine is increasingly popular, but largely confined to Managua and some of the larger towns.

### Money

U.S. dollars are changed easily in any bank or with registered money-changers on the streets throughout Nicaragua. Travelers checks are, however, rarely exchangeable outside of Managua, although with the drive to attract tourists, facilities are likely to improve in the near future. Sterling, in cash or as travelers checks, is not accepted.

### Shopping

There is a conspicuous absence of high street shops in Nicaragua, although Managua now boasts expensive malls at Metro Centro and the Inter Plaza and several supermarket chains. Tourists are more likely to enjoy shopping with the locals in the country's fruit and vegetable markets or corner stores.

### Police

The police are usually friendly, but severely short-staffed, poorly paid and under-resourced. People have been known to pay for the gas to get the police to the scene of a crime.

# ADDRESSES AND CONTACTS

Embassy of Nicaragua
1627 New Hampshire Avenue NW
Washington, DC 20009
Tel: 202-939-6570

ACERCA
(Action for Community & Ecology in the
Rainforests of Central America)
P O Box 57
Burlington, VT 05402
Tel: 802-863-0571
E-mail: acerca@sover.net
Website: www.nativeforest.org

Campaign for Labor Rights
1247 E Street
Washington, DC 20003
Tel: 541-344-5410

Global Exchange
2017 Mission Street Suite 303
San Francisco, CA 94110
Tel: 415-255-7296
Fax: 415-255-7498
E-mail: info@globalexchange.org
Website: www.globalexchange.org

Just Act
Youth Action for Global Justice
333 Valencia Street Suite 101
San Francisco, CA 94103
Tel: 415-431-4204
Website: www.justact.org

Nicaraguan Network & Education Fund
1247 E Street SE
Washington, DC 20003
Tel: 202-544-9355
Fax: 202-544-9359
E-mail: nicanet@igc.org

Quest for Peace
P O Box 5206
Hyattsville, MD 20782-0206
Tel: 301-699-0042
E-mail: quest@quixote.org
Website: www.quixote.org
(development funding and humanitarian aid)

Witness for Peace
1229 15th Street NW
Washington, DC 20005
Tel: 202-588-1471
E-mail: witness@witnessforpeace.org
www.witnessforpeace.org
(organizes 8-10 study tours to Nicaragua a year)

Embassy of Nicaragua
Vicarage House
Suite 31, 58-60 Kensington Church St.
London W8 4DB
U.K.
Tel. 0171 938 23 73

## Bookstores
The best bookstores are all found in Managua.

HISPAMER has its main outlet a few blocks west of the Central American University (UCA) and has a small branch in the campus itself. El Parnaso is opposite and the Libreria Rigoberto López Pérez is in the Centro Comercial.

## Other Websites
www.nicarao.org.ni: A non-profit server, which works to promote progressive civil society organizations in Nicaragua and Central America

www.ibw.com.ni: A commercial server providing good links to a wide variety of sites including Nicaraguan government departments and newspapers

# FURTHER READING

Belli, G. *The Inhabited Women*, New York, 1995

Black, G. *Triumph of the People*, London/New York, 1981

Cabestrero, T. *Minister of God, Ministers of the People*, London 1984

Cabezas, O. *Fire from the Mountain: The Making of a Sandinista*, London 1985

Cardenal, E., *Music of the Spheres*, London, 1990, & *Abide in Love*, New York, 1996

Collinson, H. (ed) *Women and Revolution*, London, 1990

Freeland, J. *A Special Place in History*, London, 1988

Harris, R. & Vilas, C.M. *Nicaragua: A Revolution Under Siege*, London/Boston, 1985

Haslam, D. *Faith in Struggle: The Protestant Churches in Nicaragua and their Response to the Revolution*, London 1987

Lafeber, W. *Inevitable Revolutions: The United States in Central America*, New York, 1984

Mejía Godoy, C & L.E & Castillo, J.V. *The Nicaraguan Epic*, London 1989

Melrose, D. *Nicaragua—The Threat of a Good Example?* Oxford 1985

Ramirez, S. *Stories*, London/New York, 1986 & *To Bury Our Fathers*, London/New York, 1985

Randall, M. *Sandino's Daughters Revisited*, New Jersey, 1994

Rushdie, S. *Jaguar's Smile: A Nicaraguan Journey*, London/New York, reprint 1997

Smith, H. *Nicaragua: Self-determination and Survival*, London, 1993

# FACTS AND FIGURES

## *GEOGRAPHY*

*Official name*: República de Nicaragua
*Situation*: Bordered by Honduras to the north and Costa Rica to the south, 13 00 N, 85 00 W
*Surface area*: 49,985 sq miles
*Administrative divisions*: The country was divided into nine regions by the Sandinista government. They are known by their numbers with the exception of the South Atlantic Autonomous Region (RAAS) and the North Atlantic Autonomous Region (RAAN). However, older province names are also still used. (See map)
*Capital*: Managua: (est. population 820,000, 1995)
*Other large towns*: (population x 1,000, 1995)
Matagalpa 365; Chinandega 348; León 330; Masaya 236; Estelí 169; Granada 153
*Infrastructure*: Nicaragua is almost entirely dependent on its roads for transport. There were 1,060 miles of paved roads and an estimated 9,560 miles of unpaved roads in 1995. Rivers are extremely important on the Atlantic Coast. The Escondido River is a vital link between Rama and Bluefields in the RAAS. Puerto Corinto and Puerto Sandino on the Pacific Coast are the largest ports. A limited rail network was closed in 1994. There is one international airport in Managua and three other airports in Bluefields, Puerto Cabezas and the Corn Islands on the Atlantic Coast.
*Relief and landscape*: A wide plain dominated by agriculture on the western coast, mountainous upland in the central area (the center of coffee production), and tropical forest on the Atlantic Coast.
*Climate*: Tropical. On the Pacific coast May is the hottest month, with average daily temperatures between 27 and 32°C, or 80 and 90°F.

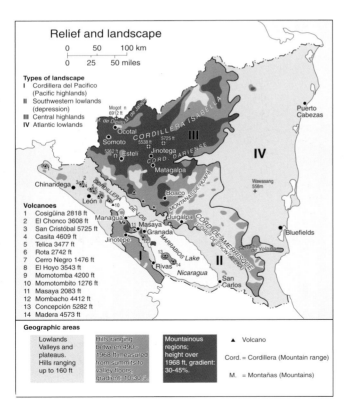

Relief and landscape

0   50   100 km
0   25   50 miles

**Types of landscape**
I   Cordillera del Pacifico (Pacific highlands)
II  Southwestern lowlands (depression)
III Central highlands
IV  Atlantic lowlands

**Volcanoes**
1   Cosigüina 2818 ft
2   El Chonco 3608 ft
3   San Cristóbal 5725 ft
4   Casita 4609 ft
5   Telica 3477 ft
6   Rota 2742 ft
7   Cerro Negro 1476 ft
8   El Hoyo 3543 ft
9   Momotomba 4200 ft
10  Momotombito 1276 ft
11  Masaya 2083 ft
12  Mombacho 4412 ft
13  Concepción 5282 ft
14  Madera 4573 ft

**Geographic areas**

Lowlands Valleys and plateaus. Hills ranging up to 160 ft

Hills ranging between 490 - 1968 ft measured from summits to valley floors; gradient: 10-30%.

Mountainous regions; height over 1968 ft, gradient: 30-45%.

▲ Volcano

Cord. = Cordillera (Mountain range)

M. = Montañas (Mountains)

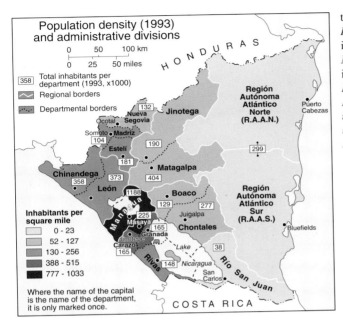

Population density (1993) and administrative divisions

| 0 | 50 | 100 km |
| 0 | 25 | 50 miles |

358 Total inhabitants per department (1993, x1000)

~~ Regional borders

···· Departmental borders

Inhabitants per square mile

- 0 - 23
- 52 - 127
- 130 - 256
- 388 - 515
- 777 - 1033

Where the name of the capital is the name of the department, it is only marked once.

tetanus, polio and measles
*Doctors*: 82 per 100,000 inhabitants
*Nurses*: 56 per 100,000 inhabitants
*Literacy*: 65.7% (1995)
*Education*: 77% enrolled at primary school and 47% at secondary school
*Social Development Index (UNDP Human Development Index 1998)*: 126th out of total 175 positions
*Religion*: 73% of the population are Roman Catholics and an estimated 16% belong to Protestant denominations

*Languages*: Nicaraguan Spanish, Miskito, Creole English and Rama, although it is now spoken by very few people

## POPULATION

*Population*: 4.5 million (1998)
*Urbanization*: 63% of population lives in urban areas (1998)
*Population growth*: 2.6% (1998)
*Fertility*: On average a Nicaraguan woman has 3.85 children (1998)
*Age structure*: 44% are under 15 years of age (1998)
*Average life expectancy*: men 65.8, women 70.6 (1998)
*Infant mortality (under 5)*: 42 per 1,000 live births (1998)
*Maternal mortality rate*:

160 per 100,000 live births (1995)
*Malnutrition among children under 5*: 12%
*Unsatisfactory water supplies*: 61%
*No access to health services*: 17%
*Unsatisfactory sanitation*: 69%
*Daily per capita calorie consumption*: 2308 (compared with 2411 in 1970 and UN recommended level of 3000)
*Immunization*: Almost 90% of children are immunized against tuberculosis and 80% against diphtheria,

Ethnic make-up of the Atlantic Coast

| 0 | 50 km |
| 0 | 25 miles |

- Miskito
- Mayangna
- Creoles (Afro-Nicaraguan)
- Garífuna (Afro-Caribbean)
- Rama

## NICARAGUA AND THE UNITED STATES/BRITAIN

The U.S. is Nicaragua's most important trading partner by far. 32% of the country's imports come from the U.S. and 42% of its exports are destined for the U.S. Nicaragua qualifies for duty-free access to the U.S. under the Generalized System of Preferences and is a member of the Caribbean Basin Initiative. Along with the other Central American countries, it aspires to joining the North American Free Trade Agreement (NAFTA). Relationships between Nicaragua and the U.S. were broken off during the 1980s, but were resumed after the defeat of the FSLN in 1990, since which time the U.S. has provided $1.2 billion in assistance, largely earmarked for debt relief and balance-of-payments support.

Trade between Nicaragua and Britain is almost non-existent. Small amounts of government aid reach Nicaragua directly through British NGOs and indirectly through the European Union.

Sources: UNDP, Economist Intelligence Unit

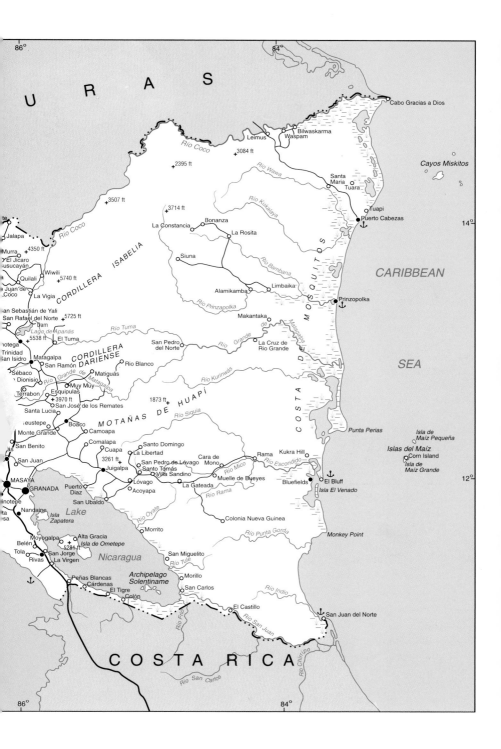

## HISTORY AND POLITICS

*Key historical dates*: * 2000 BC: earliest known indigenous settlements * 1502: Christopher Columbus lands in Central America at Cape Gracias a Dios * 1522: Spanish expedition into Nicaragua led by Gil González Dávila marks the beginning of the subjugation of Indian tribes and colonization of the region, which was incorporated into the Spanish territory of the Kingdom of Guatemala * 1589: English and Dutch pirates make bases at Bluefields and Pearl Lagoon * 1638 Kingdom of Mosquitia officially recognized by the English Crown * 1783: Britain forced to withdraw from Atlantic Coast under Treaty of Paris * 1821: Spain withdraws from Central America and the provinces of its colonial administration declare independence * 1823: Nicaragua, El Salvador, Guatemala, Honduras and Costa Rica form a federal state; United States sends gunboats to San Juan del Norte to challenge British involvement on the Atlantic Coast * 1834: slavery abolished in Nicaragua * 1838: Nicaragua declares itself an independent republic; violent conflict between Conservative and Liberal forces * 1840s: Britain returns to Atlantic Coast and makes the Miskito Kingdom a British Protectorate * 1849: Nicaragua awards the U.S. the exclusive right to build an inter-oceanic canal in return for protection against foreign aggressors * 1855: American adventurer William Walker invades Nicaragua and brings down Conservative government * 1856: William Walker becomes President of Nicaragua after holding fraudulent elections and reintroduces slavery * 1857: National War against William Walker * 1860: Britain under pressure from the U.S. to withdraw from the Atlantic Coast signs the Treaty of Managua and abandons its claim to the region * 1894: Atlantic Coast incorporated into Nicaragua by President José Santos Zelaya * 1911: U.S. asserts control over the Nicaraguan economy through the Dawson Accords * 1912: U.S. marines intervene in Nicaragua to crush a peasant uprising and remain until 1933 * 1927-1932: Augusto Sandino leads successful military campaign against U.S. interests; his forces occupy central, northern and eastern Nicaragua * 1932: newly elected President Juan B. Sacasa opens negotiations with Sandino * 1933: Sandino signs peace agreement and his forces disarm * 1934: Sandino assassinated on the orders of Anastasio Somoza, Chief of the National Guard * 1937: Somoza installs himself as president * 1956: Anastasio Somoza assassinated by Rigoberto López Pérez; his eldest son, Luis Somoza, takes over as president * 1961: FSLN founded * 1967: defeat of FSLN guerrilla unit at Pancasán in northern Nicaragua; Luis Somoza dies and Anastasio, his younger brother takes power * 1969: FSLN publishes its "historic program" which provides a framework for a future revolutionary government * 1972: earthquake destroys Managua and kills an estimated 20,000 people * 1974: introduction of martial law * 1978: Pedro Joaquín Chamorro, editor of *La Prensa* assassinated by the National Guard * 1979: FSLN takes the country's largest towns and marches victorious into Managua; Somoza and the National Guard flee * 1980: national literacy campaign; U.S. begins funding the Contras; Anastasio Somoza Jr. assassinated in Paraguay * 1983: conscription intro-

# NICARAGUA

| | |
|---|---|
| 0 ——— 50 km | |
| 0 ——— 25 miles | |
| —·——·—·— | International border |
| **MANAGUA** | Capital |
| ◉ | Cities with more than 1 000 000 inhabitants |
| ● | Towns with 80 000 - 200 000 inhabitants |
| • | Towns with 5 000 - 40 000 inhabitants |
| ○ | Towns with fewer than 5 000 inhabitants |
| ——— | Inter-American Highway |
| ——— | Major roads |
| ～～✦ | River (with dam) |
| + | Summit (heigh in feet) |
| ⊥⊥⊥⊥ | Swamp |
| ✈ | International airport |
| ⊥ | Port |

duced as Contra war intensifies * 1984: Nicaragua's first democratic elections won decisively by FSLN * 1986: Iran-Contra scandal breaks * 1987: Nicaragua's new constitution promulgated; launch of the Arias peace plan * 1989: Contras given 90 days to disarm in exchange for elections and a resettlement program * 1990: elections won by the United National Opposition (UNO); Violeta Chamorro is the first woman president in country's history * 1994: Extended Structural Adjustment Fund (ESAF I) agreement signed; Sergio Ramirez resigns from the FSLN and sets up the Sandinista Renovation Movement (MRS) * 1996 Elections won by the Liberal Alliance. Arnoldo Alemán becomes president * 1998: Extended Structural Adjustment Fund (ESAF II) agreement signed; Hurricane Mitch wrecks the economy, thousands killed * 2000: elections for local mayors, vice-mayors and councilors * 2001: elections for

president, vice-president and the National Assembly

*Constitution*: Unicameral National Assembly of 90 members and any unsuccessful presidential and vice-presidential candidates who receive over 1.1% of national vote. Twenty deputies to the assembly are elected by a system of proportional representation, in which those receiving the highest percentage of the vote at a national level are returned. 70 deputies are elected to represent the provinces. 1987 constitution reformed in 1995 to reduce the executive branch's power in favor of the legislative. President's period in office reduced from six to five years, re-election of incumbent president prohibited and provision is made for a second election when no candidate wins 45% of vote in the first round.

*Main political groupings (with seats in the National Assembly after 1996*

*elections)*: Alianza Liberal (42), Frente Sandinista Liberación Nacional – FSLN (38), Camino Cristiano Nicaraguense – CNN (5), Partido Conservador de Nicaragua – PCN (3), Proyecto Nacional – PRONAL (2), Others (3)

*Membership of international organizations*: United Nations and UN organizations, Organization of American States (OAS), Inter-American Development Bank (IDB), the Central American Common Market (CACM), the Central American Bank for Economic Integration (CABEI) and the World Trade Organization (1995)

*Media and communications*: one state-owned and six privately owned television stations, four daily newspapers (*La Prensa, El Nuevo Diario, Barricada* and *La Tribuna*) and 114 radio stations

*Telephone ownership*: 2.9 per 100 inhabitants (1995)

## ECONOMY

*Unit of currency*: Córdoba
*Exchange rate 1998*: US$1 = C$11 (December 1998)
*Gross Domestic Product (GDP)*: $1.9 billion (1995)
*Per capita GDP*: $452, second poorest nation in hemisphere

*GDP growth*: 5%, 1997
*Unemployment*: 53.2% of the economically active population are unemployed or underemployed
*Exports*: US$607 million, 1996
*Imports*: US$1,188 million,

1996
*Principal trading partners*: United States, other Central American countries, Canada, Germany
*Foreign debt*: US$11 billion, 1994; US$6.3 billion, 1998